EVERYDAY

BARBECUE

EVERYDAY
BARBECUE

At Home with
America's Favorite Pitmaster

MYRON MIXON

with **Kelly Alexander**

BALLANTINE BOOKS TRADE PAPERBACKS / NEW YORK

Published in the United States by Ballantine Books, an imprint of
The Random House Publishing Group, a division of Random House, Inc., New York.
BALLANTINE and colophon are registered trademarks of Random House, Inc.

Food photographs and photographs of Myron Mixon by Alex Martinez, copyright © 2013
by Alex Martinez; photograph on pg. xvi by Corey Shelton, courtesy of Corey Shelton.

Library of Congress Cataloging-in-Publication Data

Mixon, Myron.

Everyday barbecue / Myron Mixon with Kelly Alexander.

pages   cm

Includes index.

ISBN 978-0-345-54364-6 (pbk.)—ISBN 978-0-345-54365-3 (ebook)

1. Barbecuing.   I. Alexander, Kelly.   II. Title.

TX840.B3M58 2013

641.7'6—dc23

2012049200

Printed in the United States of America

www.ballantinebooks.com

2 4 6 8 9 7 5 3 1

Book design by Susan Turner

I DEDICATE THIS BOOK TO MY MOTHER, GAYE MIXON (GAYE GAYE), WHO ALONG WITH DAD POINTED ME NOT ONLY IN THE DIRECTION OF WHAT GREAT FOOD IS, BUT ALSO SET A HIGH STANDARD ON HOW TO BE A GOOD PERSON. THE SECOND PART I'M STILL WORKING ON.

———————

SECOND, MY MOTHER-IN-LAW, EVELYN GOODROE (BIG E), MY BIGGEST SUPPORTER, WHO BELIEVED IN ME REGARDLESS OF THE OBSTACLES THAT I ENCOUNTERED.

———————

THIRD, MY FRIEND AND BUDDY JACK (JACKLEG), AN ENGLISH BULLDOG WITH A LOOK AND DEMEANOR THAT MOST PEOPLE WOULD DO WELL TO HAVE. HE GAVE UNCONDITIONAL LOVE.

contents

CONTENTS

CONTENTS

CONTENTS

CONTENTS

MAKE IT EASY

'm Myron Mixon from Unadilla, Georgia. The winningest man in barbecue. The baddest pitmaster there ever was.

I make my living winning barbecue cooking competitions across the country. I've been doing this for nearly twenty years. It's led me to having my own line of barbecue smokers for professionals and home enthusiasts and my own brand of rubs and sauces; to be the judge of the hit show *BBQ Pitmasters* on Discovery Communications Destination America; and to be the chef/owner of the Pride and Joy Bar B Que restaurants in Miami and New York City (see page xx). I've never had a problem sharing my secrets to cooking great barbecue: I do it several times a year at Jack's Old South Cooking School, and I did it in my *New York Times*–bestselling cookbook *Smokin' with Myron Mixon*.

So, having done all of this, what do I do next?

I have one mission. I want to teach one lesson and one lesson only about cooking barbecue: Make it easy on yourself. Barbecue is simple food. People come up to me all the time and ask me the same question over and over: **"How** can I cook barbecue in my backyard if I don't have a smoker like yours?" My answer: I could cook great barbecue with a handful of coals and a trash can. (I actually proved this when I was on the *Late Late Show with Craig Ferguson*.) I learned to barbecue the old-fashioned way, in hand-dug pits, from my daddy, Jack Mixon, and I didn't design a big ole cooker like the kind I use now until I'd already won a few cooking contests and could afford to. Today I design and build all my own cookers, but you don't need anything fancy to make great barbecue. You can do it on the smoker or grill you already have in your backyard, or even in the oven in your home. You just need to know what you're doing, and I'm going to show you.

The first thing you need to know is that **barbecue isn't special occasion food; it's everyday food.** It doesn't have to take all day to cook, and it sure doesn't have to be complicated.

Now, if you want my championship-winning recipes for traditional barbecue favorites, including my world-famous, often imitated but never equaled whole hog, you should buy a copy of my first cookbook. But can you make most of those recipes in half an hour on a Tuesday night? No, you cannot. But that doesn't mean that there aren't easier, quicker ways to achieve great barbecue, and I'm here now to show them to you.

If you wonder what I know about making dinner, let me tell you how it is. See, I don't just cook when I'm trying to win a pork shoulder competition in Kansas City or Memphis (see Memphis Barbecue Network, page xxi). What a lot of people don't realize about me is that I don't have a "side job" like most people on the barbecue circuit: I don't have a building contracting business, I don't own a car lot, and I sure as hell don't sell insurance. I am a professional cook, and so I'm always cooking. I live and breathe and even sleep and dream barbecue. I have to: To keep winning competitions, my recipes need to be constantly evolving and getting better.

So I'm perpetually thinking about recipes, and always experimenting in the kitchen, too. When I'm not on the road, you're just as likely to find me grilling a steak on my patio as you are to see me worrying over a brisket in my smoker in my laboratory, or—as I like to call it—the Billion-Dollar Barbecue Pavilion, I erected in my backyard. This book is more about what I do on the patio than what I do when I'm smoking meat for competition.

I'm giving you those recipes that I rely on in my everyday life. These are the Grilled Pimento Cheese Sandwiches (page 65), the Baby Back Mac and Cheese (page 203), and the Chocolate Cake on the Grill (page 265) I make for dinner for my own family. I've got recipes in here that will positively knock your socks off: The King Rib (page 48), for example, is the best sandwich ever invented.

I'm here to tell you: Nothing in this book is particularly time-consuming to cook. That's because I'm here to prove to you that you can cook on your barbecue every single night of the week if you want to. I like fast cooking and I don't like worriation, and I think most home cooks are probably a whole lot like me when it comes to those two things.

There are three special chapters in here that I want you to look at if you feel like doing something a little different, breaking from the norm, if you will:

My **DRUNKEN RECIPES** chapter is all about showing you that if you use a little bit of whiskey in your cooking, you raise its flavor profile and add a level of interest to your food that will make whatever you're cooking about 100 percent tastier. Make my Bourbon-Bacon Burger (page 159) and you'll see what I mean.

My **BARBECUE-FRIED** chapter is a personal favorite: For years I've been ruminating on how to combine my two favorite cooking techniques, and I've come up with a roster of recipes that show you why it's such a good idea: Try my Barbecue-Fried Baby Backs (page 116) and you've got the recipe for your next kitchen addiction.

My **LEFTOVERS** chapter reflects growing up in a household where nothing was wasted, my daddy made sure of that. We canned and preserved in the summer, we fished for our Friday night suppers, and we collected wood for the smokers. Knowing how to make use of leftovers separates the men from the boys in the kitchen: You got to know how to take one meal and turn it into two. You want your mind blown: Turn straight to the Baby Back Mac and Cheese recipe (page 203). That's the best leftovers creation there is.

Listen, you're busy, you've got to get dinner on the table, so you'd better get to it. Go ahead, fire up your grill and see how easy it is to make a meal no matter how little time you've got. You can thank me later.

You know what I do when I'm not cooking at home? Lately I've been opening restaurants, and let me tell you that Pride and Joy is one of the highlights of my career. For me it's the culmination of everything that I've been working on in the barbecue world: I learned barbecue cooking at my daddy's knee; I picked up my family's barbecue sauce business to help support us after my father passed away; then I started competing on the professional barbecue circuit (and winning every contest I entered); then came television and my first cookbook. In nearly all of these endeavors, I felt like I was chasing my father's larger-than-life legacy, working hard to do right by him and make him and my family proud. I worried, though, that along the way I was getting further away from the very reason my father cooked barbecue in the first place: to feed his people.

Yes, I sell my award-winning sauces and rubs, giving people access to my food in that way, and I share my recipes in my cookbooks. But I realized what I wanted was my own restaurant. Not just any restaurant. Back home in Unadilla and its surrounding towns I've run various small barbecue joints, places where you can get pulled pork sandwiches and rib plates, and that has been rewarding. But spots like that are a dime a dozen in the South; every neighborhood has one, if not two, and they're almost always pretty good. What I wanted to do was something bigger and badder: I wanted to prove that barbecue isn't just food for small-town Southerners. It's delicious enough to play in the big leagues. Hell, good barbecue is for everybody.

My original Pride and Joy opened in Miami in November 2012, and it's been a huge hit: Packed crowds have helped me realize the goal of bringing my brand of barbecue to a big city; this is my chance to serve the people who have been watching me win from their living rooms all these years. For my next challenge, I'm going to show New Yorkers what great barbecue tastes like. My second Pride and Joy restaurant opened in the spring of 2013 and is the best barbecue in the Big Apple. Come see me for a plate of Baby Back Mac and Cheese, a pile of the world's winningest smoked brisket, and a King Rib when you're in town.

THE MEMPHIS BARBECUE NETWORK

If there's a professional organization I'm positively passionate about, it's the Memphis Barbecue Network (MBN). There are three major groups that produce, organize, and run barbecue contests in America: the Kansas City Barbeque Society (KCBS), the International Barbeque Cookers Association (IBCA), and the Memphis Barbecue Network. I have love for all of them, and I've won money and top prizes in contests officially sanctioned by all three.

The reason MBN holds a special place in my heart is because they sanction the Big Pig Jig in my backyard of Vienna, Georgia, a contest that my daddy helped found and that helped me get my start cooking on the big circuit. I also love the MBN because it's the only contest network that allows teams to cook whole hogs, and that to me is the true test of a barbecue champion. Contests like this one remain truest to the traditions of Southern barbecue and are among the most important to the real competitors out there. The MBN sanctions all-pork contests all over the country. Their judging is based on six criteria: area and personal appearance, presentation (including verbal explanation of your cooker, your team, and your cooking methods), appearance of the entry, tenderness of the entry, flavor of the entry, and overall impression. All but the first two of these categories are judged blind. This is a hell of way to run a contest, as thorough as it can be. I like that you have to be able to cook the best damn pork shoulder, ribs, and whole hog *and* that you have to be able to interact professionally with the certified judges.

I fight against the perception that a barbecue contest cook is someone who sits back in a camper for a weekend with some friends and drinks a few cocktails while he smokes a hog shoulder and sees who wins the money. I take barbecue contests seriously, and so does this organization. I'm proud to help promote what the MBN stands for: a contest with integrity. And I sure do like winning, naturally. Come out and see me do it at any of the number of competitions I attend each year.

one

HOW IT'S DONE

Remember this, folks: My job here in this book is to show you that barbecue is food that you can enjoy every day. I'm going to break it down and make it as easy as possible for you to make at home.

Six different cooking methods work for the recipes in this book:

1. Grilling on a charcoal grill
2. Grilling on a gas grill
3. Smoking on a smoker
4. Smoking on a charcoal grill
5. Smoking on a gas grill
6. Using an oven

Now I don't want to confuse you with too much information up front. So what I'm going to do is offer up a general primer right here, right now, and give you all the steps you need to adapt just about any recipe in this book to whichever your preferred cooking method may be. And along the way if there's additional information you need about cooking methods, I'll give it to you then and there.

HOW TO READY A CHARCOAL GRILL

Spread coals on the bottom of the grill.

Using lighter fluid: Pour the lighter fluid on the coals as directed in the instructions, and move away from the grill before you strike the match.

With a chimney starter: These are the very popular 6- to 8-inch-wide cylindrical canisters with handles attached that make good fire starters. To light charcoal (or wood, either way), place a few sheets of newspaper or some lighter-fluid-touched charcoals in the bottom of the grill. Place the chimney on the charcoal grate, fill with charcoal or wood, touch a lit match to the newspaper or charcoals, and the coals will begin to blaze. When most of the coals are white-hot, lift the chimney and dump out the coals into the base of the grill.

Spread the hot coals on the bottom of the grill. It may take up to 30 minutes to get to 500°F (for high heat). Use the hand-pass test to determine the heat: For medium-high heat, rake the coals into a slightly thinner layer and let them burn 5 to 10 minutes longer, so your hand can linger over the coals comfortably for about 5 seconds (count to 5 slowly: one-one-thousand, two-one-thousand, etc.); if you can make it to five without having to pull your hand away, the temperature is right. For medium heat, spread the coals even wider along the bottom of the grill and do the hand-pass test for 7 to 8 seconds. For medium-low heat, let the coals burn for 10 to 15 minutes longer than you did for medium-high. You should be able to hold your hand six or so inches above the hot coals for 10 seconds.

The last thing to do before laying your meat on the grill: Make sure your grill grate is clean. The kettle itself can be smoke-and-spice seasoned, a condition that imparts another layer of flavor onto your meat, but you need for that actual grate to be pretty free of encrusted leftovers. When the grill is heating and you've already lit the coals, it's in its "preheated" state: First, brush the grate with a long-handled wire brush. Then use a spatula to scrape off any pieces of debris. Now oil the grates, and there are two methods that work for me. In a hurry: Using heavy-duty potholders, carefully remove the cleaned grate from the grill and spray it with nonstick cooking spray or some olive oil from one of those misting canisters. A little more time: Leaving the grate on the grill, take a couple of sheets of folded-over paper towels, dip them in about ¼ cup vegetable oil to coat, and, grasping the oil-soaked paper towels with tongs, rub them up and down the bars of the hot grate.

HOW TO READY A GAS GRILL

Set all burner dials on high. Preheat until the temperature reaches 500°F. This usually takes 10 to 15 minutes. For medium-high, preheat the grill to high, then turn the burner dials down to medium-high. The temperature should read about 400°F. For medium, preheat the grill to high, then turn the burner dials to medium. The temperature should read about 350°F. For medium-low, preheat the grill to high, then turn the dials down to medium-low. The temperature should read about 325°F.

HOW TO PREPARE A SMOKER FOR SMOKING

Smokers are made for smoking, but there is a wide range of options from the charcoal-burning "bullet"-style smokers to the ceramic Big Green Egg. In any of these you need to choose which wood you'll smoke, and I recommend fruit woods because they're mild in flavor, and high in sap, and generally have fewer impurities in them; you can choose from whatever is easiest to find near you: apple, cherry, grape, and my personal favorite, peach. Soak your wood chips an hour before you plan to light your smoker. Start your charcoal in a charcoal chimney as described above. Place the coals in the bottom third of the smoker (the firebox). Scatter the pre-soaked wood chips on the coals. What I want you to do that you may not already know about is to put a pan of water in the bottom of your smoker. A water pan is not a requirement to cook barbecue; it's a stylistic touch that I like. I like it because it has a significant benefit: The water pan creates a steamy water bath inside the smoker that helps maintain the meat's moisture, which is found naturally in its marbling (or fat). The water helps maintain a moist juicy texture in the meat and prevent it from drying out. To set up a water pan, simply fill a medium heavy-bottomed pan (no bigger than a 13 by 9-inch lasagna pan) about halfway with water and place it in the bottom of your smoker. The grill racks (there are usually two) fit above the water pan. Close the lid and monitor the fire until it reaches your desired temperature.

HOW TO PREPARE A KETTLE OR
OTHER CHARCOAL GRILL FOR SMOKING

Take about a cup of your favorite wood chips (I like peach wood, being from Georgia) and soak them in enough water to cover them for at least an hour or, even better, overnight. When you're ready to cook, drain the wood chips. Wrap them in aluminum foil and seal the edges; the best description I've seen of this technique is to make it like a "burrito"—a packet of soaked and drained wood chips. Using a long wooden skewer or a sharp-tined fork, poke several holes in the top of the packet. Set the packet aside. Then prepare the grill: On a standard kettle grill, bank your charcoal to one side, leaving a cold area for the meat to be placed (an "indirect" heat area, where the meat is not directly over the flame but is still being cooked by it). Then place that packet of wood chips underneath the charcoal. Place the lid on the kettle and control the level of the heat with the kettle grill's vents, opening them up more to cool the smoker and closing them to raise it.

HOW TO PREPARE A GAS GRILL FOR SMOKING

Most models of gas grills have either two or three burners that can be controlled individually. Here's what you do: Take about a cup of your favorite wood chips (I like peach wood, as I mentioned above) and soak them in enough water to cover them for at least an hour or, even better, overnight. When you're ready to cook, drain the wood chips. Wrap them in aluminum foil and seal the edges; the best description I've seen of this technique is to make it like a "burrito"—a packet of soaked and drained wood chips. Using a long wooden skewer or a sharp-tined fork, poke several holes in the top of the packet. Set the packet aside. (Make 2 if you have a 3-burner grill.) On a two-burner gas grill, light only one side; on a three-burner unit, light the two outside burners and leave the middle one cold. Place the packet of wood chips on the lit section (or sections). The flame will smolder the wet chips, producing smoke to cook and flavor your meat. Then you will place your meat on the unlit section of the gas grill and cook it with indirect heat. That's it. Don't worry about the grill's side vents and making them closed airtight; do the best you can to shut them, but don't worry; none of my smokers are what you'd call "airtight" either. And I win money with my food all the time.

INDIRECT VERSUS DIRECT HEAT

You will hear me talking about "indirect" and "direct" heat throughout this book. Direct heat is simple: The food is cooked directly over the heat source. Food is cooked fast and hot— like my Perfect Grilled Rib Eyes (page 83) or my Mexican-Style Grilled Corn (page 245). Indirect heat means the heat source is a bit removed from the food. If the left burner is lit on your gas grill and you're cooking Myron's Dr Pepper Can Chicken (page 88) on the right side of the grill, that's cooking with indirect heat. In that case, we're not creating smoke, but if we were, we'd be smoking. Here's the important difference: We're not always smoking when we're using indirect heat, but we're always using indirect heat when we're smoking. Got it?

HOW TO USE A KETTLE OR OTHER CHARCOAL GRILL
FOR DIRECT-HEAT GRILLING

In other words, you're using high heat to cook thin (or thinnish) pieces of meat like steaks and chicken breasts, kebabs and veggies, and the grilled sandwiches and French toast in this book.

Regulating the heat is particularly important with direct grilling: Too hot and you'll char your food, too cool and you won't cook it at all. Real barbecue guys use the "hand-pass" test: Hold your hand about six inches or so over the coals. Count to three slowly (one-one-thousand, two-one-thousand), and if you can make it without having to pull your hand away, the temperature is about right for the kind of fast, hot cooking you're about to do (you're looking for about 500°F here). Direct grilling almost never requires you to close the grill, so you can stand right by your steaks and make sure they don't, God forbid, catch on fire.

HOW TO USE A KETTLE OR OTHER CHARCOAL GRILL
FOR INDIRECT-HEAT COOKING

Even if you don't plan to smoke something, if you're making something large on the grill—a whole chicken, say, or a pork roast—you sure can't cook it at full fiery blast. What you're going to do is follow the steps above to light and prepare your grill down through oiling the grate. Then what you're going to do is bank the heated coals on either side of the grill and leave the bottom of the center of the grill empty. Next you're going to arrange the food in that center cool spot, above but between the hot coals. Then you're going to close the grill and control the temperature using the vents. The temperature you're aiming for in indirect grilling is about 350°F.

REGULATING THE HEAT IN ANY SMOKER OR GRILL

As I've said time and time again, cooking over fire is not complicated. And making sure your temperature stays consistent is very important but not very difficult after you understand how it's done.

Obvious fact #1: As charcoal burns, it cools. This starts to happen after about an hour. If you're cooking something for less than an hour, don't worry about it. If you're cooking something that requires more time than that, you'll have to do something.

Obvious fact #2: When you're using a smoker or a grill for indirect-heat cooking, you're going to need to replenish the coals about every hour, or every time the grill temperature dips 50 or more degrees below what you need it to be.

Obvious fact #3: This is as easy as watching the temperature, opening the grill, adding the new coals near some already well-lit ones, and making sure they catch fire. Monitor the cooker's temperature and then add your new coals when necessary, and you'll be able to maintain a consistent temperature in your cooker.

MYRON'S BACKYARD BARBECUING TIPS

When you're smoking and grilling, don't open the lid if you don't have to. Every time you open it, you lower the temperature inside it by about five degrees or so—and it'll take several additional minutes of cooking time to make up for that loss of heat. In using a grill and a smoker, maintaining consistent temperature is very important.

Make your life easier with aluminum foil baking pans. Now some folks in the world of barbecue look down their noses at cooks like me who use aluminum foil to wrap meats and who put meat in aluminum pans. They don't think this is "authentic" enough—cavemen didn't have foil, that's their attitude. Well, cavemen didn't have satellite television either, and I do. I use aluminum pans because they're the easiest ways to convey meat from the house to the smoker and then from the smoker to the table. They keep the meat from falling apart, which you risk when you transfer it from a prep station to a smoker, and they make cleanup a whole lot easier.

Use charcoal and lighter fluid to start your fire. I don't know about you, but I don't have a whole lot of time to waste rubbing sticks together to get a so-called natural fire burning. On the barbecue circuit I'm a "stick burning competitor," which means I cook meat over smoking whole sticks of wood, which I believe flavors it like nothing else. However, I start my fires with charcoal to get a blaze going to burn the wood, and I start the charcoal with lighter fluid. Some of my fellow competitors protest and scrutinize this method, saying it makes the meat taste like lighter fluid. That's only true if you don't read the damn directions on the bottle of fluid about how to use it. After you apply a small amount of lighter fluid to coals, don't do anything until the coals burn white. Then the fluid has burned off, and you've started your fire as easily as possible while still having the benefit of cooking over real wood.

Let your meat rest after you pull it off the grill or smoker. Transfer your beef, chicken, lamb, or pork from the grill or smoker to a cutting board, loosely cover it with foil, and let it rest for at least a few minutes before getting into it and serving it. This seals the juices in and keeps the meat from drying out. Do not cut until you are ready to immediately serve and eat it. Keep those juices flowing till the last minute—you'll thank me.

two

THE LUCKY THIRTEEN
THE ESSENTIALS

THE ONLY MARINADE YOU NEED

THE ONLY BARBECUE RUB YOU NEED

THE ONLY OTHER BARBECUE RUB YOU NEED

THE ONLY BARBECUE SAUCE YOU NEED

THE ONLY OTHER BARBECUE SAUCE YOU NEED

THE BASIC PORK BUTT, NO IFS, ANDS, OR BUTTS

PORK SHOULDER THE EASY WAY

BRISKET THE EASY WAY

BARBECUE WHOLE CHICKEN THE EASY WAY

RIBS THE EASY WAY

COLESLAW, THE ONLY SIDE DISH YOU NEED

CORNBREAD, THE ONLY OTHER SIDE DISH YOU NEED

GRILLED FRUIT CRISP, THE ONLY DESSERT YOU NEED

Yes, it's true that I'm a champion competitive barbecuer—you knew that already, and in fact it's probably why you are reading this. But what you may not know is that when I'm home on the weeknights and my off days, I'm not usually smoking a whole hog, checking the clock every fifteen minutes to make sure I'm spritzing my ribs at the proper intervals, or wrapping my briskets in blankets. For details of those methods you'll have to read my first book, *Smokin' with Myron Mixon,* where I give you the kind of recipes that require extra time and effort to prepare and perfect.

When I'm cooking to win hearts rather than dollars, I rely mostly on the following thirteen recipes—my "lucky thirteen," if you will—so I can kill two birds with one stone: Serve my guests a delicious barbecue meal, and try not to let any of my friends or family members drive me crazy while I enjoy it. I'm sure it's the same for you; when you're relaxing at home and putting together dinner, you don't want to deal with the worriation of a multiple-step, highly involved smoking process. You want to serve delicious food but also spend time with friends and family. I get it, believe me.

This chapter includes my most basic, reliable, and trusted recipes, the ones I use in my own downtime. Here are my tried-and-true formulas for barbecue classics, the dishes we all crave—smoky pink-tinged brisket, mouthwatering ribs, tangy pulled pork. I give you a perfect marinade, a perfect rub, and a perfect sauce (or two, because I'm just that nice). You can use the recipes in this section as jumping-off points, and I encourage you to make them your own: Do you like the warmth and depth of cumin in your rub? Go ahead and add a pinch or two in there. Prefer a tangy bite in your coleslaw? Feel free to spike my recipe with a little apple cider vinegar. These recipes are the secrets to barbecuing quickly and well, but I've designed them in such a way that you don't need to follow them precisely. Use them as guidelines, get comfortable with how truly easy barbecue cooking is, and you'll be making great meals in no time. That's my barbecue philosophy: It's a simple food, don't mess it up.

Remember: My goal here is to show you that you can enjoy good barbecue every day of the week. Now, I can't do the impossible: Some of these recipes require a little extra planning up front—for Ribs the Easy Way (page 35), you'll almost definitely need to visit a butcher counter, for instance—but the reward is that when you get ready to make dinner, it's going to be a no-fuss process and it's going to taste damn good too.

FOR BEEF

Marinate big cuts like brisket, beef tenderloin roast, prime rib roast, and eye of the round or top round roast for at least 6 hours or, preferably, overnight.

Marinate steaks like porterhouse, T-bone, or New York strip for 30 minutes before cooking while you prepare the rest of the meal (steaks can stay in the marinade for up to 2 hours).

FOR CHICKEN

Marinate wings, breasts (bone-on or boneless), **legs,** and any other pieces you like to cook for at least 2 hours or overnight.

Marinate a whole bird (in a deep pan) overnight.

FOR PORK

Marinate pork shoulder and pork loin roasts for 4 hours.

Marinate pork tenderloin for at least 30 minutes or up to 2 hours.

The Only Marinade You Need

For Pork, Beef, Chicken, and Anything Else You Want to Marinate

What's the job of a marinade? Simple: To infuse flavor onto and into your meat, and to tenderize it in the process. Why do I call this "the only marinade you'll ever need"? Because even though in barbecue competitions I have all different sorts of marinades for different meats and I am always working on new ways to layer flavor into smoked meat, at the end of the day when you're cooking dinner in your backyard for your family—as I often am—you need a simple go-to marinade you can count on for just about anything. This is it, and it's damn delicious.

Makes 1 quart

3 cups apple juice
1 cup distilled white vinegar
¾ cup sugar
¾ cup kosher salt

In a large, heavy saucepan, combine the apple juice and vinegar and whisk over medium heat. Whisking continuously, pour in the sugar and salt. Continue whisking until the seasonings are completely dissolved, but do not allow the mixture to come to a boil. Remove the pan from the heat and cool completely. If reserving for a later use, use a funnel and pour the marinade into a large bottle or container. You can store this marinade in a tightly covered container in the refrigerator for up to 1 year.

> *I MARINATE EVERYTHING IN AN ALUMINUM PAN COVERED IN THE REFRIGERATOR, AND I ADVISE YOU TO DO THE SAME.*

The Only Barbecue Rub You Need

For Pork, Beef, and Anything Else You Want to Throw on the Grill

What does a rub do? Its job is to season the meat, help seal in moisture, and ensure you get great flavor on your smoked and grilled meats. Do you have to use it? No, of course not. You're the cook, and sometimes a steak is great with just salt and pepper, but it's a really easy thing to make ahead of time and keep around, and it makes your food taste exponentially better—so a rub is worth making and having in your bag of tricks. That said, if you're lazy, buy my own brand from me directly at jacksoldsouth .com. (Hey, don't you think I've forgotten for a second about my first love: making money!) Or you could try this recipe, which approximates (but never equals, mind you) my own secret formula.

Makes just under 2 cups

1 cup packed light brown sugar
2 tablespoons chili powder
2 tablespoons mustard powder
2 tablespoons onion powder
2 tablespoons garlic powder
2 teaspoons cayenne pepper
2 tablespoons kosher salt
2 tablespoons freshly ground black pepper

In a large bowl, combine all the ingredients. Stir thoroughly to combine. You can store this rub in an airtight container for up to 1 year.

The Only Other Barbecue Rub You Need

For Chicken, Fish, Seafood, Veggies, and Light Foods

Do you need more than one rub? Technically you do not. That said, it's nice to look at the natural character of what you're cooking and tailor your spices accordingly. I like this rub here for lighter meats like chicken and fish, which are more subtle and delicate in flavor and could become overwhelmed by particularly spicy rubs.

Makes 2 cups

⅔ cup chili powder
½ cup sugar
¼ cup kosher salt
¼ cup onion powder
¼ cup garlic powder
1 teaspoon cayenne pepper

In a large bowl, combine all the ingredients. Stir thoroughly to combine. You can store this rub in an airtight container for up to 1 year.

The Only Barbecue Sauce You Need

For Pork, Beef, and Anything Else You Pull off the Grill

I have heard people eating barbecue at festivals say that "the sauce makes the barbecue." It's not true. The smoke makes the barbecue. The sauce is a finisher. It's what you put on your meat after it cooks to enhance its appeal. It can add a great punch, but I've had plenty of delicious barbecued meat with no sauce at all. I've been around barbecue sauces of different stripes all of my life. My family's sauce recipe, which my parents were just beginning to market when my father suddenly passed away, is what got me into cooking competitive barbecue in the first place. We have always preferred a hickory-style sauce, meant to closely evoke and complement the flavor of hickory-smoked meats. It's world famous and a secret recipe, so the only way you'll taste the original is to order it from me, but if you insist on not giving me your business, here's a reasonable approximation that is still damn delicious.

Makes about 3 cups

2 tablespoons onion powder

2 tablespoons garlic powder

Two 6-ounce cans tomato paste

2 tablespoons paprika

⅔ cup cider vinegar

2 tablespoons Worcestershire sauce

¼ cup packed dark brown sugar

2 tablespoons honey

2 tablespoons maple syrup

2 tablespoons kosher salt

2 tablespoons freshly ground
   black pepper

Combine all of the ingredients in a blender and pulse a couple of times to thoroughly combine. Pour the mixture into a medium saucepan and place over medium heat. Stir continuously until the sauce is heated through, but do not allow it to come to a boil. Remove the pan from the heat. Use the sauce immediately as you like, or, if reserving for a later use, allow the mixture to cool, then pour it into a large bottle or container and store, tightly covered and refrigerated, for up to 1 year.

The Only Other Barbecue Sauce You Need

For Chicken, Fish, Shrimp, and Anything Else You Pull off the Grill

The different types of sauce is the great barbecue regional debate, but as a personal preference, I really like the vinegar-based Eastern North Carolina style of barbecue; it's got a bright, bracing flavor that pairs so well with smoked foods. Since it's vinegar based and not tomato, it is clearer and thinner than what some people may be used to. It's also near addictive.

Makes about 3½ cups

2 cups cider vinegar

1 cup tomato puree

½ cup Louisiana-style hot sauce or other favorite hot sauce

2 tablespoons kosher salt

2 tablespoons freshly ground black pepper

1 tablespoon red pepper flakes

½ cup sugar

Combine the vinegar, tomato puree, and hot sauce in a medium saucepan and place over medium heat. Pour in the remaining ingredients and stir to dissolve, but do not bring to a boil. Remove the pan from the heat. Use the sauce immediately as you like, or, if reserving for a later use, allow the mixture to cool, then, using a funnel, pour it into a large bottle or container and store, tightly covered and refrigerated, for up to 1 year.

The Basic Pork Butt, No Ifs, Ands, or Butts

The pork "shoulder" is what butchers have for years called the top of the front leg of the hog. It's not exactly a shoulder. It actually has two parts: the lower portion, called the "picnic" or "picnic ham," and the upper part, called the "Boston butt" or the "Boston blade roast," which is from the area near the loin and contains the bone. This cut is what most pulled pork sandwiches are made with. It's ideal for smoking because, even though it's an inexpensive and muscle-packed cut, it's well marbled and full of fat and becomes velvety tender when you cook it right—which is what I'm about to show you. Note that a shoulder with both Boston butt and picnic ham attached as one piece of meat may have to be ordered ahead of time from a butcher because in many supermarkets the cuts are pre-separated.

Serves 30 to 40

One 15- to 20-pound pork shoulder, including the Boston butt and picnic ham in
   one cut
1 recipe Only Marinade (page 21)
1 recipe Only Rub (page 22)
1 cup Only Sauce (page 24) for serving

Take a moment to run your fingers over the shoulder, feeling for any protruding bits of bone. Using a sharp knife, trim off any of these bone slivers from the exposed meat, and cut off any visible excess fat.

Place the shoulder in a plastic 10-gallon-size bag. Pour in the marinade and knot the bag. Let the shoulder sit in the refrigerator for at least 4 hours or overnight.

Prepare a smoker with soaked wood chips and heat it to 250°F (see page 6). Alternatively, prepare a charcoal grill (see page 7) or gas grill (see page 8) for smoking and heat it to high heat.

Take the shoulder out of the marinade and pat it dry with paper towels. Sprinkle the rub all over it, making sure to cover as much surface as possible. Place the shoulder in an aluminum pan. Cover the pan with aluminum foil and place it in the smoker or on the grill. Cook for 6 hours, or until the internal temperature reaches 205°F.

Remove the pan from the smoker or grill. Allow the meat to rest, covered, for 30 to 45 minutes before serving. Put on heavy-duty gloves and pull the meat apart in chunks. Discard the gloves and, using tongs, pile the pulled pork on guests' plates or sandwich buns. (Before serving you can chop up the pork chunks after you've pulled them, if you like.)

Make it in the oven: Preheat the oven to 300°F. Marinate the pork as directed above. Remove the pork from the marinade and discard the marinade. Pat the pork dry with paper towels. Sprinkle the rub all over it, making sure to cover as much surface as possible. Place the shoulder in an aluminum pan. Place the pan in the oven and cook for about 6 hours, basting well with the pan juices every hour, until it collapses and yields easily to the pressure of a fork. When the meat is done, remove it from the oven and let it rest, covered, for at least 30 minutes and up to 1 hour. Pull the meat apart as directed above. Serve with Only Sauce on the side.

Pork Shoulder the Easy Way

This is the world's easiest way to make barbecued pork. I achieve it by cutting out all but the most necessary steps: There's no brining, no injecting, and there's not even a bone. If you want to make barbecue pork quickly, get yourself a boneless roast. This recipe is excellent for a weeknight party or a small, hassle-free backyard birthday party, and it should give you enough leftovers for sandwiches the next day.

Serves 10 to 12

One 6- to 8-pound boneless pork shoulder butt (blade roast)
1 recipe Only Marinade (page 21)
1 cup Only Rub (page 22)
1 cup Only Sauce (page 24) for serving

Place the shoulder in a large aluminum baking pan, add the marinade, and marinate in the refrigerator for at least 1 hour or, if you can, overnight.

Prepare a smoker with soaked wood chips and heat it to 550°F (see page 6). Wait at least 15 minutes, so the temperature lowers to about 300°F. Alternatively, prepare a charcoal grill (see page 7) or gas grill (see page 8) for smoking and heat it to high heat.

Remove the meat from the marinade and discard the marinade. Pat the meat dry with paper towels. Apply the rub all over the meat. Place the roast in an aluminum pan fat side down, place in the smoker or grill, and smoke uncovered for 4 to 4½ hours, until the pork reaches an internal temperature of 195°F. Remove the pork from the smoker, cover it with aluminum foil, and let it rest for 30 minutes (it will continue to cook when it's off the heat, raising the internal temperature to 205°F). Pull the pork, chop it, or slice it as you wish and serve immediately with sauce on the side.

Make it in the oven: Preheat the oven to 300°F. Marinate the meat as directed above, and remove the meat from the marinade. Discard the marinade and pat the meat dry with paper towels. Apply the rub all over the meat. Place the roast in an aluminum pan fat side down, place in the oven, and roast uncovered for 4 to 4½ hours, until the pork reaches an internal temperature of 195°F. Remove the pork from the oven, cover with aluminum foil, and let it rest for at least 30 minutes and as long as 1 hour (it will continue to cook when it's off the heat, raising the internal temperature to 205°F). Pull the pork, chop it, or slice it as you wish and serve immediately with Only Sauce on the side.

Brisket the Easy Way

The best way to save time on smoking a brisket is easy; buy a small one that will cook faster! I have to use big ones for competition, but buying one that has already been cut and trimmed can save a lot of time. What you ideally want is a 5-pound flat-cut brisket, a perfect size for a family dinner. After cooking all different types of brisket—from generic grocery store chain varieties to the most expensive cuts money can buy—I prefer wagyu, which is meat that comes from a type of cattle by that same name. Wagyu beef is beautifully marbled, really rich in flavor, and especially tender and juicy—it's also expensive, so if you don't have the time (or the funds) to source it, save it for a special occasion and get the best flat-cut 5-pound brisket you can find (local sources of meat are always good to use anyway). No matter what you get, it's going to be delicious because you're cooking it my way.

Serves 8

One 5-pound trimmed flat-cut brisket
2 cups Only Marinade (page 21)
¾ cup Only Rub (page 22)
2 cups Only Sauce (page 24), for serving

Place the brisket in an aluminum pan. Pour the marinade over it. Cover and refrigerate for at least 6 hours or, preferably, overnight.

Thirty minutes before you are ready to cook the brisket, heat a smoker to 350°F (see page 6). Alternatively, prepare a charcoal grill (see page 7) or gas grill (see page 8) for smoking and heat it to high heat.

Remove the brisket from the marinade and discard the marinade. Let the meat come to room temperature and then, with your hands, apply the rub all over the meat. Place the brisket in a clean aluminum pan, place the pan in the smoker, and cook uncovered for 1 hour. Remove the pan from the smoker and cover it with aluminum foil. Put it

continued

back into the smoker and cook for another 30 to 45 minutes, until the temperature registers 205°F.

Remove the pan from the smoker and let it rest at room temperature for 30 minutes.

Remove the brisket from the pan and slice it against the grain; try to make the slices as consistently sized as possible. Place the slices on a warm platter and pour the brisket's pan juices over them. Serve immediately.

Make it in the oven: Preheat the oven to 350°F. Marinate the brisket as directed above. Remove the brisket from the marinade and discard the marinade. Let the meat come to room temperature and then, with your hands, apply the rub all over the meat. In a very large enameled cast-iron casserole, heat 3 tablespoons vegetable oil. Add the brisket and cook over medium-high heat, turning, until browned all over, about 12 minutes. Pour 2 cups of chicken stock or water into a large aluminum baking pan. Using tongs, carefully transfer the brisket into the prepared pan. Cover with aluminum foil and roast in the oven for 1 hour. Remove the foil, baste the brisket, and continue to roast for another 30 minutes, or until the internal temperature registers 205°F. Carefully transfer the brisket to a carving board and let rest for 30 minutes. Carve and serve immediately, with Only Sauce on the side.

Barbecue Whole Chicken the Easy Way

You need exactly two things to make this succulent, smoky bird: the bird and the rub. It's a hearty, humble pleasure: a guaranteed easy dinner for a busy weeknight or thrown-together family-style barbecue (and I know, because I often serve it on the first "welcome" night of my cooking school). If you like sauce on the chicken, put it on after you cook it so it doesn't smother the flavor—and choose a light, vinegar and red pepper flake–based version like my Only Other Sauce.

Serves 4

1 small whole chicken, about 3½ pounds
1 recipe Only Other Rub (page 23)
1 cup Only Other Sauce (page 25), optional

Prepare a smoker with soaked wood chips and heat it to 275°F (see page 6). Alternatively, prepare a charcoal grill (see page 7) or gas grill (see page 8) for smoking and heat it to high heat.

Wash the chicken thoroughly and pat it dry with paper towels. Apply the rub all over the exposed area of the chicken and into the chicken's cavity as well. Place the seasoned chicken breast side up on a meat rack with the handles down so the bird will be raised above the surface of the pan. Set the rack inside a deep aluminum baking pan. Pour 2 cups of water into the pan, underneath the meat rack. Place the pan in the smoker and cook, covered, for about 3 hours, or until the breast meat reaches a temperature of 165°F and the dark meat reaches 180°F.

Remove the pan from the smoker and allow the chicken to rest on its rack in the pan uncovered for 15 minutes. Transfer the chicken to a carving board, carve the chicken into pieces, and serve with the Only Other Sauce.

Make it in the oven: Preheat the oven to 425°F. Prepare the chicken as directed above. Set the aluminum pan in the oven and roast for about 1 hour, until the juices run clear when an inner thigh is pierced. Transfer the chicken to a carving board and let rest uncovered for 10 minutes. Cut the chicken into pieces and serve with the Only Other Sauce.

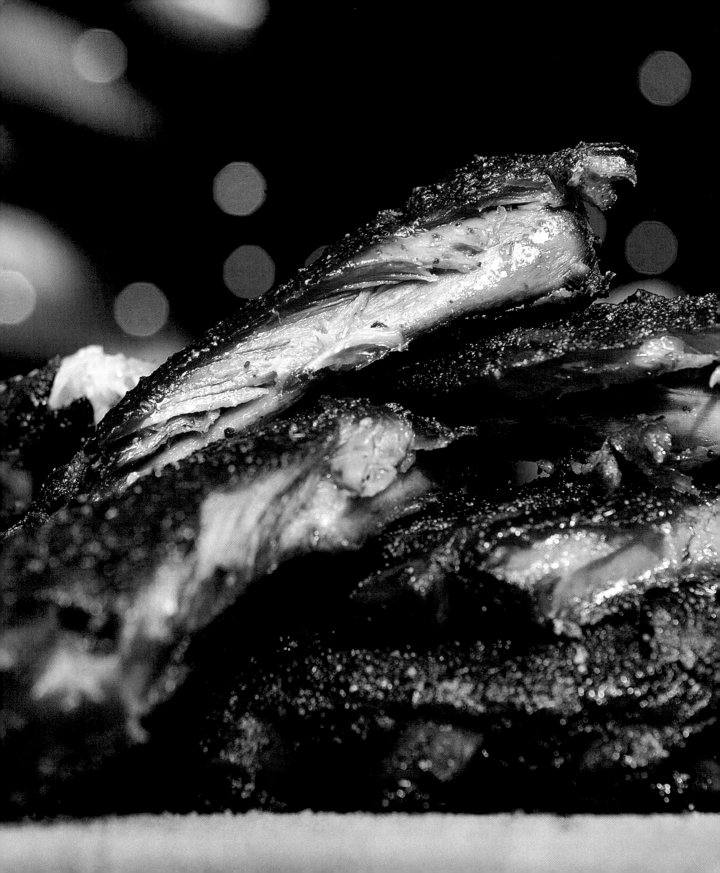

Ribs the Easy Way

The first thing you have to do to make ribs the easy way is to go to a butcher counter—and every grocery store in the world has one if you don't feel like making a special trip to a designated butcher shop—and ask for "Kansas City–style ribs." These are spareribs—the long bones from the lower part of the hog's belly behind its shoulder—and they're an inexpensive, easy-to-find cut in any supermarket deli counter. What makes them "Kansas City–style" is the fact that they have the breastbone and skirt removed: In other words, they're trimmed as much as they possibly can be, with no membranes or excess fat—a perfect rectangle of meat and bone, and thus extremely easy and less time-consuming to handle and cook. Taking the extra time at the butcher counter and letting the trained professional trim your meat is going to save you a lot of hassle at your barbecue.

Serves 8 to 12

4 racks Kansas City–style spareribs
1 recipe Only Marinade (page 21)
1 recipe Only Rub (page 22)
1 recipe Only Sauce (page 24)

Set the racks of ribs in an aluminum baking pan and cover them completely with the marinade. Cover the pan with aluminum foil and refrigerate for at least 4 hours or overnight.

When you are ready to cook the ribs, remove them from the marinade. Pat them dry with paper towels. Apply the rub lightly around the edges of the ribs, over the backs of them, and on top. Then let the ribs sit uncovered at room temperature for 30 minutes.

Prepare a smoker with soaked wood chips and heat it to 275°F (see page 6). Alternatively, prepare a charcoal grill (see page 7) or gas grill (see page 8) for smoking and heat it to high heat.

continued

Put the ribs in a clean aluminum baking pan, uncovered (so the ribs can absorb as much smoke as possible), put it in the smoker, and cook for 3 hours.

Remove the pan from the smoker. Pour 1 cup of water into a clean aluminum pan. Place the ribs in the pan bone side down and cover the pan with aluminum foil. Place the pan in the smoker and cook for about 2 more hours.

Remove the pan from the smoker and shut off the heat on the smoker. Remove the foil and apply the sauce to the top and bottom of the slabs of ribs. Re-cover the pan with foil, return it to the smoker, and let the ribs rest in the smoker, covered, for about 1 hour as the temperature gradually decreases.

Remove the ribs from the pan and let them rest for 10 minutes uncovered on a wooden cutting board. Cut the ribs to separate them and serve.

Make them in the oven: You will need 2 additional cups of Only Sauce for the oven method. Prepare the ribs as directed above. Preheat the oven to 350°F. Line 2 rimmed baking sheets with foil and place a wire rack on top of each. Transfer 2 racks of ribs to each wire rack meat side up. Place the sheets in the oven and roast, switching positions of baking sheets about halfway through, until the meat pulls away easily from the bones, 1½ to 2 hours. Raise the oven temperature to 425°F. Brush both sides of the ribs with the 2 cups sauce. Roast until the sauce is slightly caramelized, about 15 minutes. Remove from the oven. Let the ribs stand for 5 minutes, then cut to separate them; serve with more sauce.

Coleslaw, the Only Side Dish You Need

What goes great with smoky, sweet-tangy, chile-spiked meats? A cold, creamy, and crunchy side dish. This is why coleslaw has been barbecue's most important accompaniment since man started cooking with fire. I've got a couple of exciting ways to make both slaw and cabbage (I love it smoked; see Barbecue Smoked Cabbage, page 254), but if you're throwing a barbecue for a crowd and you don't want to be bothered with trying something new, use this foolproof formula. You can prepare it up to 6 hours in advance and store it, covered, in the refrigerator. But *do not add the salt* until right before you're ready to serve the slaw—and toss it again just before serving—or it will become watery!

Serves 12

2 medium heads green cabbage, coarsely chopped into thin strands
2 sweet onions, preferably Vidalia, diced
2 ripe tomatoes, diced
2 cups mayonnaise
Kosher salt
Freshly ground black pepper

In a large bowl, combine all of the ingredients. Toss thoroughly. Serve immediately.

Cornbread, the Only Other Side Dish You Need

If you're going to fire up your smoker, you need some cornbread to sop up the sauce on the plates. You can add whatever you like to this basic batter—grated sharp cheddar cheese, whole corn kernels, diced red peppers, maybe even some cracklin' bacon bits—but it'll work just perfectly on its own.

Serves 6

1 cup all-purpose flour
1 cup yellow cornmeal
2 teaspoons kosher salt
1 large egg, beaten
1 cup whole milk

Preheat the oven to 425°F.

Sift the flour, cornmeal, and salt into a large bowl. Stir in the beaten egg and milk and mix until the batter is relatively smooth; it will remain a little lumpy, and that's fine. If the mixture seems dry, add a tablespoon or two of water to moisten it.

Pour the batter into a greased 8-inch cast-iron skillet or 8-inch square baking pan. Bake until the top is golden brown and a tester inserted into the middle of the cornbread comes out clean, 20 to 25 minutes.

Remove the cornbread from the oven and allow it to cool in the pan on a wire rack for 10 minutes, then cut into wedges and serve.

Grilled Fruit Crisp, the Only Dessert You Need

When I've got the grill going I like to take advantage of it by making the entire meal on it—including dessert. Yes, I'm one of those folks who like to have a little something sweet to round out the meal. I came up with this fruit crisp as a go-to dessert that I can quickly assemble in a cast-iron skillet and then set on the heat. It can be filled with just about any fruit you like, such as ripe peaches in the summer or tart apples in the fall.

Serves 6

¼ cup plus 2 tablespoons all-purpose flour
¼ cup plus 2 tablespoons light brown sugar
¼ cup plus 6 tablespoons granulated sugar
6 tablespoons cold unsalted butter, cut into small pieces
1 cup coarsely chopped pecans
½ cup old-fashioned rolled oats
2½ pounds fruit, such as Granny Smith apples or Georgia peaches, peeled, quartered, cored or pitted, and sliced crosswise ¼ inch thick
½ cup dried cranberries (or dried blueberries or cherries, or a combination)
Ice cream or whipped cream for serving, optional

In a food processor, pulse the flour with the brown sugar and ¼ cup of the granulated sugar until combined. Add the butter and pulse until the mixture resembles coarse meal. Transfer the crumbs to a bowl and stir in the chopped pecans and oats.

Generously butter a large cast-iron skillet. In a medium bowl, toss the fresh fruit with the cranberries and the remaining 6 tablespoons sugar. Pour the fruit mixture into the prepared skillet and cover with the topping.

If you do not already have a hot grill going, heat a charcoal grill (see page 10) or gas grill (see page 8) set up for indirect heat to 350°F.

Set the skillet on the cool side of the grill. Cover the grill and cook until the fruit is tender and bubbling and the topping is browned, 45 minutes to 1 hour. Remove the skillet from the grill and let rest for 10 minutes. Serve warm, with ice cream or whipped cream if you like.

Make it in the oven: Preheat the oven to 350°F. Prepare the crisp as directed above. Set the skillet on a rack in the bottom third of the oven and bake for 45 to 50 minutes, until the fruit is tender when pierced and the topping is browned. Serve warm, with ice cream or whipped cream if you like.

three

BURGERS AND SANDWICHES

THE KING RIB

THE CLASSIC HICKORY-SMOKED BARBECUE BURGER

BRISKET CHEESESTEAKS

BACON-WRAPPED CHICKEN BURGERS

SMOKED TURKEY BURGERS

LAMB BURGERS WITH FETA, ONION, AND TOMATO

BARBECUE PORK AND SLAW BURGERS

SPICY SALMON BURGERS

GRILLED SMOKED SAUSAGE, PEPPER, AND
   CARAMELIZED ONION HOAGIES

BARBECUE PORK BELLY SLIDERS

GRILLED PIMIENTO CHEESE SANDWICHES

BARBECUE BOLOGNA SANDWICHES

BACON-WRAPPED HOTDOGS

GRILLED REUBEN BRATS

GRILLED CHICKEN SANDWICHES

GRILLED TUNA SANDWICHES

SMOKED BACON BLTS

BARBECUE VEGGIE SANDWICHES

Knowing how to make a delicious hamburger is a basic life skill. Who doesn't like a good old-fashioned juicy burger? Maybe you're watching your weight, or your cholesterol, or you're a vegetarian or a damn vegan, but still you know what you want in a burger. Whoever you are, I bet you like some kind of burger, some way, somehow.

I'm going to give you a whole bunch of ideas for how you can do burgers easily on the grill any old time you feel like it. You want your burger to have a hint of the fiery intensity that only cooking on a barbecue can give it. Then you can put whatever you like on there. I'm sticking with Jack's Old South hickory sauce. And maybe a slice of smoked bacon or two. That's the Myron Mixon way.

But there are several other burgers in this chapter that you should try, like the Bacon-Wrapped Chicken Burgers (page 54) or the pork, turkey, lamb, and salmon versions. All of them are delicious. You'll also enjoy some new greats like Grilled Pimiento Cheese Sandwiches (page 65) or the melt-in-your mouth Barbecue Pork Belly Sliders (page 62), and my barbecue spin on classics like Brisket Cheesesteaks (page 52) and Grilled Tuna Sandwiches (page 71).

Beyond the burger and sandwiches, though, at the top of this chapter is the only sandwich you'll ever need. For a crowd pleaser, you should look no further than the King Rib (page 48). Take my award-winning baby back ribs, sliced off the rack, heaped onto a soft roll, topped with onions, and you'll be the backyard barbecue champion you deserve to be.

The King Rib

This is truly a sandwich fit for a king. There's a version out there that some fast-food chain serves, and it has become a cult favorite. Mine will make women and children weep—and grown men, too. You can make this with my baby back ribs (Barbecue-Fried Baby Backs, page 116) or using leftover rib meat. Either way, you simply cannot beat it.

Note: The most important step in this process is cutting the meat off the bone so that you have the kind of flat, long piece that you need for this sandwich. You can use hot-off-the-grill baby backs or leftovers.

Makes 4 sandwiches

1 pound leftover baby back rib meat (horizontally cut off the bones from 1 rack)
1 cup Only Sauce (page 24)
Four 6-inch sandwich rolls or buns, split
8 dill pickle slices
½ cup finely chopped sweet onions, such as Vidalia
Garnish and condiments of choice

Once you've got the cut of meat, reserve it, wrapped in foil, in the refrigerator until you're ready to use it. When you're ready to make the sandwiches, cut the meat into 4 equal portions. Then warm the meat on a baking sheet in the oven, in a toaster oven, or in a large skillet until it's hot, 3 to 4 minutes on each side in a 350°F oven or in a pan over medium heat.

Pour the sauce into a large, shallow bowl. When the pork is thoroughly heated, use tongs to dip each piece of meat into the sauce to completely cover with sauce on both sides. Lay one pork piece on the bottom of each roll. Arrange 2 slices of pickles on top of the pork. Scatter 2 tablespoons of the onions over the top of the pickles and pork. Cover each sandwich with the top of the roll. Serve immediately or, if you like, micro-wave each sandwich for 15 seconds to give it that "fresh from under the fast-food lights" heat.

The Classic Hickory-Smoked Barbecue Burger

People talk about "thirty-minute meals," and I'm thinking, "I can make a delicious dinner in ten." And this is how. Note that I like a big, juicy burger: If you don't, instead of four big burgers, make six smaller ones. Either way, don't handle the meat too much: The looser it is packed, without falling apart, the juicer the burger becomes. You want to just combine it with the mustard and the rub so that the flavors are worked in properly, but don't overhandle it or you'll get a tough burger. Have a light touch, move quickly, and you've got yourself dinner.

Makes 4 to 6 burgers

1½ pounds ground beef, preferably ground chuck with at least 20% fat, at room
    temperature
2 teaspoons Dijon mustard
1 tablespoon Only Rub (page 22)
Salt and freshly ground black pepper
4 to 6 hamburger buns, split
2 tablespoons unsalted butter, melted
3 tablespoons Only Sauce (page 24)
Garnish and condiments of choice

Heat a charcoal grill (see page 4) or gas grill (see page 5) to medium-high heat.

In a medium bowl, combine the beef with the mustard and rub, gently kneading into 4 to 6 equal patties, about ¾ inch thick each. Season the burgers very generously with salt and pepper and transfer to a plate lined with plastic wrap. Brush the cut sides of the buns with the melted butter.

continued on page 51

Grill the burgers directly on the grill for about 10 minutes, turning once, for medium. Move the burgers away from the heat to rest on a warm (but definitely not hot) part of the grill and grill the cut sides of the buns for about 1 minute, until toasted.

Brush the tops and bottoms of the buns with the sauce.

Slide the burgers onto the buns and top them with lettuce and tomato and whatever toppings you prefer. Serve immediately.

Brisket Cheesesteaks

The Philly cheesesteak is a classic sandwich made with very thinly sliced beef sautéed with onions and piled on a hoagie with cheese. It's just a no-brainer to give leftover brisket the same treatment. Remember to slice it as thinly as you can. If the meat is still firm from being in the refrigerator, it will be easier to cut (so you can refrigerate the leftovers for at least an hour before you make these sandwiches). In Philadelphia they serve it with runny and gooey Cheez Whiz, but I prefer provolone for the sharper kick.

Makes 4 sandwiches

2 tablespoons olive oil
4 large yellow onions, thinly sliced
Salt and freshly ground black pepper
3 cloves garlic, chopped
1 large green bell pepper, thinly sliced
1 tablespoon Dijon mustard
2 tablespoons Worcestershire sauce
2 teaspoons Louisiana-style hot sauce
1 tablespoon all-purpose flour
1½ cups beef or chicken stock
1 large round loaf of crusty bread or 4 crusty baguette-style rolls
1½ pounds leftover smoked brisket, cut into very thin slices (see page 53)
12 slices provolone cheese

Preheat the oven to 350°F.

Heat the olive oil in a medium skillet over medium heat. Add the onions and season with salt and pepper. Cook, stirring occasionally, for 7 to 8 minutes, until the onions soften and brown. Add the garlic, bell peppers, mustard, Worcestershire sauce, and hot sauce to the pan. Continue to cook until the peppers are soft and the onions are brown in color, about 7 minutes more.

Add the flour and cook for about 1 minute, then add the stock and simmer until thickened, 3 to 4 minutes.

Meanwhile, cut the loaf of bread or rolls in half lengthwise. Scoop out some of the bread from the inside and toast the halves in the oven or a toaster oven.

Add the leftover brisket slices to the onion-and-pepper mixture in the pan and stir to combine.

Open the toasted bread or rolls and layer provolone on both sides. Top the provolone with the steak mixture and close the sandwich.

Transfer the sandwich to the oven for 2 to 3 minutes to melt the cheese. Remove from the oven, cut into wedges if using a single large loaf or in half if serving individual sandwiches, and serve immediately.

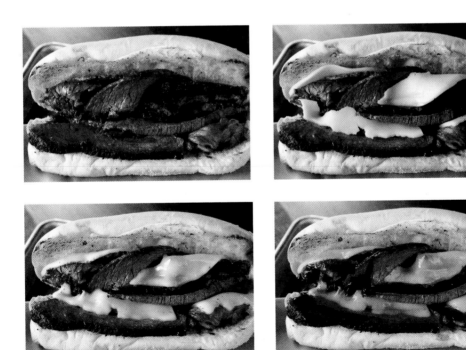

Bacon-Wrapped Chicken Burgers

What's great about a chicken burger is that *if you're careful* you can make them really moist and juicy without making them extremely fattening. And yes, I say that while I'm encouraging you to wrap yours up in a slice of bacon. The key to a good chicken burger is to infuse it with as much flavor as you can, because on its own chicken is quite mild. The hickory sauce and rub do wonders for these burgers, making them tangy and piquant, and you don't need me to tell you what bacon does—it makes everything better, of course.

Serves 2, depending on how big you like them

1 pound ground chicken
   (white or dark meat,
   or a combination)
½ cup finely chopped onions
½ cup Only Sauce (page 24)

1 teaspoon salt
1 teaspoon freshly ground black pepper
4 slices bacon (not thick cut)
1 teaspoon Only Rub (page 22)
2 onion rolls, split and lightly toasted
Garnish and condiments of choice

Heat a charcoal grill (see page 4) or gas grill (see page 5) to medium heat.

In a medium nonreactive bowl, stir together the chicken, onions, sauce, salt, and pepper until thoroughly blended. Gently form the mixture into burger patties.

Wrap each burger with a strip of uncooked bacon and secure it with a couple of toothpicks. (If you prefer very crisp bacon, precook the bacon to about half done, let it cool slightly, then wrap the burgers. With this method, the bacon shrinks somewhat, so 2 slices may be needed to surround each burger.)

Sprinkle both sides of each burger with the rub.

Grill, uncovered, for about 10 minutes or so on each side, just until the center is perfectly pink. Let the burgers rest, covered, for 10 minutes, then slide them onto the toasted onion rolls.

Dress the burgers as you like and serve immediately.

Smoked Turkey Burgers

Smoking turkey gives the bird a deep and intense flavor. I like it better than grilling it over high heat. The extra time and lower heat allows the meat to pick up a delicious smoky flavor. This is (pretty much) the reason I smoke my Thanksgiving turkeys. A good condiment is essential here, because turkey burgers can take some extra zing and need a little more wetness. Guacamole is excellent, along with a slice of pepper Jack cheese. (Note: You can turn this smoked turkey burger it into a grilled turkey burger simply by preparing the meat, then cooking it on a hot grill over direct heat for about 5 minutes per side.)

Makes 2 burgers, depending on how big you like them

¼ cup minced green onions
1 garlic clove, minced
1 teaspoon Worcestershire sauce
Salt and freshly ground black pepper
1 pound ground turkey (dark or white meat, or a combination)
2 hamburger buns, lightly toasted
Garnishes and condiments of choice

Prepare a smoker with soaked wood chips and heat it to 300°F (see page 6).

In a medium nonreactive bowl, stir together the green onions, garlic, Worcestershire sauce, and salt and pepper to taste. Add the turkey, gently combining it with the mixture, and form it into patties. The burgers may be prepared up to this point, covered, and refrigerated up to 1 day ahead.

Place the burgers in a shallow aluminum pan and place the pan in the smoker. Cover and cook for about 15 minutes for medium-rare (and up to 30 minutes for medium-well to well done).

Serve the burgers on the toasted buns with your favorite garnishes and condiments.

Lamb Burgers with Feta, Onion, and Tomato

We don't have a lot of Greek food in Unadilla, Georgia—or really any—but I love the flavors and the tradition of cooking lamb over an open spit. It reminds me of the kind of old-fashioned smoking my dad, Jack Mixon, used to do and that I rarely get the opportunity to do these days since I'm on the road so much. Plus, I've had plenty of experience cooking lamb in various Kansas City Barbecue Society contests, some of which have "mutton" as a category—so I got pretty good at cooking it, because you know I'm not going to leave any money on the table.

Serves 2, depending on how big you like them

1 pound ground lamb
⅓ cup packed crumbled feta cheese
1 teaspoon dried oregano
1 teaspoon salt, plus more for the onions
1 teaspoon freshly ground black pepper, plus more for the onions
2 large garlic cloves, peeled and finely diced
2 tablespoons extra-virgin olive oil
1 small red onion, peeled and thinly cut crosswise
2 teaspoons virgin olive oil
2 hamburger buns, split
1 small tomato, thinly sliced

Heat a charcoal grill (see page 4) or gas grill (see page 5) to medium-high heat.

Break up the lamb into a large bowl. Sprinkle in the feta, oregano, salt, pepper, garlic, and extra-virgin olive oil; toss gently with your hands to combine. Divide into 2 equal portions and form each into a patty, pressing in the center to form a slight indentation. Set aside.

Brush the onion slices with the virgin olive oil and sprinkle with salt and pepper. Place the burgers and onions on the grill. Cover and cook for about 5 minutes, then turn and cook, covered, until the onions are charred in spots and the burgers are medium-well, about 4 minutes longer. Transfer to a plate. Place the buns on the grill cut side down and toast for about 1 minute. Turn and heat for about 1 minute.

Place the burgers inside the buns topped with the onion and tomato slices. Serve immediately.

Barbecue Pork and Slaw Burgers

What's great about a pork burger is a lot like what's great about a pulled pork sandwich: The fat melts into it and makes it juicy to the point of bursting with flavor. Combine that with my barbecue sauce, and it's just about the most winning combination out there. You want to make sure the burgers get nice and seared and golden on the outside. The sauce acts as a kind of glaze here, sealing in the meat's moisture and adding an additional layer of spicy-sweet flavor.

Makes 2 to 4 burgers, depending on how big you like them

1 pound ground pork
1 teaspoon salt
½ teaspoon freshly ground black pepper
3 to 4 tablespoons Only Sauce (page 24)
2 to 4 onion rolls, split and toasted
½ cup Only Slaw (page 37)

Heat a charcoal grill (see page 4) or gas grill (see page 5) to medium heat.

In a medium bowl, mix together the pork, salt, pepper, and 2 tablespoons of the sauce until combined, taking care not to overmix, then gently form the meat into patties.

Grill the patties, covered only if using a gas grill, until just cooked through, about 3 minutes per side. Brush the top of each patty with ½ tablespoon of the remaining tablespoon barbecue sauce, then turn over and grill for about 30 seconds. Brush the top of each patty with the remaining ½ tablespoon barbecue sauce, then turn over and grill for about 30 seconds more. Slide the burgers off the grill.

Lay the pork burgers in the onion rolls topped with the slaw. Serve immediately.

Spicy Salmon Burgers

I'm probably one of the only people you know who has a fondness for old-fashioned salmon croquettes, made out of canned salmon and fried up in butter. But I wanted to come up with a more modern way of doing those old croquettes, especially since so many people like to grill salmon. Also, because my mantra is all about infusing meat with smoky flavor, I thought the same treatment would work well with salmon. It's such a supple, smoothly textured fish, making it very easy to "grind" your own for very fresh burgers. Note: These burgers are much, much easier to handle if they are chilled for one hour before grilling. Take special care not to overcook them: Juiciness is the key to a good salmon burger.

Makes 2 to 4 burgers, depending on how big you like them

1 pound skinless boneless salmon fillet, cut into 1-inch pieces
1 large egg, lightly beaten
1 tablespoon fresh lemon juice
1 tablespoon Dijon mustard
¼ cup chopped green onions
1 garlic clove, minced
1 teaspoon salt
½ teaspoon freshly ground black pepper
½ cup tartar sauce
1 tablespoon dried dill
1 teaspoon grated lemon zest, optional
2 to 4 sesame seed rolls, split
Red onion slices
4 to 8 Bibb lettuce leaves

Place the salmon, egg, lemon juice, and mustard in a food processor and pulse until coarsely ground. Transfer the mixture to a medium bowl and mix in the green onions,

continued

garlic, salt, and pepper. Gently form into 2 to 4 ½-inch-thick patties. Cover and refrigerate for at least 1 hour and up to 4 hours.

Heat a charcoal grill (see page 4) or gas grill (see page 5) to medium-high heat.

In a medium bowl, whisk together the tartar sauce, dill, and lemon zest, if using.

Grill the rolls until toasted, then transfer to plates and spread the bottom halves generously with the enhanced tartar sauce. Grill the salmon patties uncovered until the fish is cooked through, about 2 minutes per side. Place the burgers atop the sauce on the rolls. Top each with onion slices, 2 lettuce leaves, and the top half of the roll. Serve immediately.

Grilled Smoked Sausage, Pepper, and Caramelized Onion Hoagies

A sausage-and-pepper hoagie is something most people associate with old-fashioned Italian-style delis in places like New York and Chicago. Good stuff; I'm not arguing with it. But I make a barbecue version: My sausage-and-pepper hoagie uses barbecue sauce instead of marinara sauce, making it both tangier and sweeter.

Makes 4 hoagies

1½ pounds smoked sausage links (two 12-ounce packages smoked sausage)
1 red or green bell pepper, halved, cored, and seeded (or use half of each color)
Four ½-inch-thick slices red onions
¼ cup Only Sauce (page 24)
4 hoagie rolls or 8-inch French bread rolls, split

Heat a charcoal grill (see page 4) or gas grill (see page 5) to medium-high heat.

Cut each sausage link in half crosswise. Place the sausage, bell peppers, and onions on the grill and grill, covered, for 5 minutes. Turn, then continue grilling, covered, for 5 minutes, or until the sausage is heated through and the vegetables are crisp-tender.

Brush the sauce over both sides of the sausage and vegetables. Arrange the rolls cut side down around the edges of the grill. Continue grilling, covered, for about 2 minutes, until the rolls are lightly toasted. Cut the bell peppers into strips and separate the onion slices into rings.

Pile the sausage and vegetables into the rolls to make sandwiches. Serve immediately.

Barbecue Pork Belly Sliders

You know what pork belly is? It's bacon that hasn't been sliced yet. I made these pork belly sliders at the South Beach Wine & Food Festival, when I cooked there with Nadia G from Cooking Channel's *Bitchin' Kitchen,* and now they're a staple at my Pride and Joy Bar B Que restaurants. They're that good!

Makes 12 to 16 sliders

2½- to 3-pound pork belly side
3 tablespoons Only Sauce (page 24)
1 recipe Only Slaw (page 37)
½ seedless cucumber, thinly sliced
12 to 16 small potato rolls, split

Wash and then thoroughly dry the pork belly. Place the pork belly in a large zip-top bag, pour the sauce over the top, and massage it. Refrigerate for at least 4 hours or, preferably, overnight.

Prepare a smoker with soaked wood chips and heat it to 150°F (see page 6). Alternatively, prepare a charcoal grill (see page 7) or gas grill (see page 8) for smoking and heat it to medium-high heat.

Prepare the pork belly: Use a sharp knife to score the pork belly by making a few slices going in both directions across it. Place the pork belly in a medium aluminum pan. Place the pan in the smoker, cover, and let it smoke for 1 hour. Remove the pan from the smoker and let the pork belly rest, uncovered, for 10 minutes. Using a sharp knife, thinly slice the pork belly.

To assemble the sandwiches, place a slice of pork belly, some slaw, and a slice of cucumber on the bottom half of each roll. Top with the top half of the rolls and serve immediately.

Grilled Pimiento Cheese Sandwiches

A lot of people talk about *grilled* cheese, but did you ever notice how most of them are talking about sandwiches *fried* in a pan on the stovetop? How about a real grilled cheese made on a grill, touched with a little smoky flavor? Good idea. It's even better if you make it with the Southern staple known as pimiento cheese, a spread made of little more than grated cheddar, pimiento peppers, and mayonnaise. It's comfort food at its finest, and the smoke only makes it more intense. Want more? Add a slice of ripe tomato or a couple of strips of bacon—or both.

Makes 4 sandwiches (with 2 to 2½ cups pimiento cheese)

1½ cups grated sharp cheddar cheese
1½ cups grated processed cheese, such as Velveeta
One 2½-ounce jar chopped pimiento peppers, with their juice
¼ cup sugar
½ to ¾ cup mayonnaise, to taste
1 tablespoon freshly ground black pepper
8 slices sourdough bread, such as Pepperidge Farm Sourdough
Olive oil

Make the pimiento cheese: In a large bowl, combine the cheeses, pimiento peppers and their juice, sugar, mayonnaise, and pepper. Using a wooden spoon, an electric mixer at medium speed, or a food processor, blend the ingredients until well combined. Cover and chill for at least 3 hours or, preferably, overnight.

Make the sandwiches: Heat a charcoal grill (see page 4) or gas grill (see page 5) to medium-high heat.

Brush one side of each piece of bread with olive oil. Place a scoop of pimiento cheese between 2 slices of bread, oiled side out. Do not overfill, as the cheese can easily ooze out the sides while on the grill.

continued

Place the sandwiches on the grill, top with a baking sheet, and use a heavy object (such as a brick or a large canned good) to press them down. Grill for 90 seconds on one side, remove the heavy object and baking sheet, flip the sandwiches, and press again. Grill for another 90 seconds, then remove the sandwiches from the grill. Serve immediately.

Barbecue Bologna Sandwiches

My father, Jack, loved bologna, and he passed that love right on to me. It's also really big on the professional barbecue circuit, where teams make barbecue bologna sandwiches and snack on them during competitions. They even serve barbecue bologna sandwiches at the Memphis airport. Folks in Mississippi and Oklahoma like bologna so much that I've heard it described as both "Mississippi prime rib" and "Oklahoma prime rib." If your idea of bologna is some thin wet slices of mystery meat, think again: Real deli bologna is sweet and mild, perfect for heaping on a layer of smoky flavor. Note: Texas Toast is the name brand of the kind of bread this sandwich is customarily served on; for the unfamiliar, it's double-thick slices of prebuttered garlicky bread that you toast yourself in the oven, and it's addictive.

Makes 8 to 10 sandwiches

One 3- to 5-pound whole unsliced bologna (any kind will do, including kosher all-beef)
1 recipe Only Rub (page 22)
1 loaf Texas toast, sliced 1 inch thick
1 recipe Only Slaw (page 37)
1 recipe Only Sauce (page 24)

Prepare a smoker with soaked wood chips and heat it to 225°F (see page 6). Alternatively, prepare a charcoal grill (see page 7) or gas grill (see page 8) for smoking and heat it to medium-high heat.

Using a sharp knife, make a vertical cut that runs the length of the bologna but does not cut all the way through: Aim to make the slice about two-thirds of the way through the bologna. Again: Be sure not to cut it all the way through. Apply the rub to the bologna inside and out. Put the bologna in an aluminum pan and place the pan in the smoker. Cover and smoke for about 3 hours, until the bologna is mahogany in color and it reaches an internal temperature of 145°F. Let the bologna rest uncovered for 10 minutes.

Slice the bologna about ½ inch thick. Place 2 slices of bologna between 2 pieces of Texas toast, first topping with a small scoop of slaw and a drizzle of sauce. Serve immediately.

Bacon-Wrapped Hotdogs

I've heard these puppies referred to as "heart attack dogs" by people from Los Angeles, where bacon-wrapped franks are very popular and sold off of Korean food trucks. I get it: They're wrapped in bacon, and they are indeed decadent. That's why they're my favorite to serve at a backyard barbecue with friends and family.

Makes 6 sandwiches

6 all-beef hotdogs

6 slices bacon

6 thick-cut slices onion

1 red or green bell pepper, cored, halved, and seeded (or use half of each color)

1 tablespoon olive oil

2 tablespoons mayonnaise

6 hotdog buns, split

4 teaspoons mayonnaise

6 teaspoons prepared mustard

Heat a charcoal grill (see page 4) or gas grill (see page 5) to medium-high heat.

Carefully break 4 toothpicks in half. Wrap the entire length of each hotdog in a strip of bacon and secure with a toothpick half at each end. Set aside. Brush the onion slices and bell pepper halves with the olive oil.

Place the hotdogs, onions, and bell peppers on the grill. Grill until the bacon is crisp and fully cooked and the hotdogs are heated through, about 6 minutes, rotating the hotdogs several times to evenly cook the bacon and closing the grill between turnings. When the hotdogs and vegetables are done, remove them from the grill and set aside.

Evenly spread the mayonnaise inside the buns, slice each pepper half into strips, then evenly distribute the vegetables among the buns. Remove the toothpicks from the hotdogs and place a bacon-wrapped dog in each bun. Spread each dog with 1 teaspoon mustard. Serve immediately.

Grilled Reuben Brats

I can relate to the Jewish delicatessen smoked meat tradition, even though it's a bit different from my own. These grilled brats are my version of a classic Reuben sandwich, using the same ingredients but making it a bit more "barbecue" in nature. Simmering the brats in beer makes them moist and flavorful, and it also shortens their grilling time; if, however, you're short on time yourself, you can cut that step and just throw the brats on the grill.

Makes 4 sandwiches

One 12-ounce bottle beer (preferably a pale lager such as Stella Artois)
4 uncooked fresh bratwurst links (about 1 pound)
2 tablespoons Thousand Island dressing
4 buns or hotdog rolls, preferably rye, split
½ cup shredded Swiss cheese (2 ounces)
1 cup sauerkraut, drained

Heat a charcoal grill (see page 4) or gas grill (see page 5) to medium heat.

In a 2-quart saucepan, bring the beer to a boil. Add the bratwurst, reduce the heat to low, cover, and simmer for 15 minutes.

Drain the bratwurst and place it on the grill. Cover the grill and cook for 5 to 10 minutes, turning once, until browned.

Spread the dressing on the cut sides of the rolls. Place the bratwurst in the rolls and top with the cheese and sauerkraut. Serve immediately.

Grilled Chicken Sandwiches

You can find a generic, average, ho-hum, plain old grilled chicken sandwich at just about every restaurant in America. And I get the appeal of them. But, I got to wondering, how could I add a little *Myron* to the grilled chicken sandwich? And by "Myron," I mean, how can I add something that's going to make this sandwich worthy of cash and prizes, of praise and adoration? Here's what I came up with, and it's one damn good chicken sandwich.

Makes 6 sandwiches

¼ cup plus 2 tablespoons olive oil
1 tablespoon Only Rub (page 22)
Twelve ½-inch-thick chicken breast cutlets (2½ pounds)
6 onion rolls, split
Salt and freshly ground black pepper
2 lemons, cut into 3 wedges each
3 tablespoons Only Other Sauce (page 25)
Garnishes: pepper Jack cheese slices, lettuce leaves, tomato slices

In a large bowl, whisk ¼ cup of the olive oil with the rub. Spoon 1½ tablespoons of the mixture into a medium bowl, add the chicken, and turn to coat. Let the chicken stand in the marinade at room temperature for 30 minutes.

Heat a charcoal grill (see page 4) or gas grill (see page 5) to high heat.

Brush the rolls with the remaining 2 tablespoons olive oil and grill until golden. Add the chicken to the grill, season with salt and pepper, and grill uncovered, turning once, until cooked through and lightly charred, about 6 minutes. Remove the chicken from the grill. Squirt fresh lemon juice from the wedges onto each breast, then allow the chicken to rest uncovered for 10 minutes.

Spread the sauce on the cut sides of the rolls. Place 2 chicken cutlets inside the rolls, topping with the cheese, lettuce, and tomatoes before you close the sandwiches. Serve immediately.

Grilled Tuna Sandwiches

I love the fact that tuna is a lot like steak but healthier and faster to grill, two excellent attributes for a fast-cooking and delicious recipe. My tuna sandwich is a hybrid: It combines some traditional tuna flavorings such as soy sauce with the flavors of barbecue—I use rub and sauce in this recipe—which makes my tuna fish sandwich unlike any you've tried before.

Makes 4 sandwiches

2 tablespoons soy sauce

1 tablespoon vegetable oil

1 tablespoon apple juice

1 teaspoon Only Other Rub (page 23)

4 tuna steaks, about 4 ounces each

2 tablespoons mayonnaise

1 tablespoon Only Sauce (page 24)

4 kaiser rolls or sandwich buns, split

Lettuce leaves

1 large tomato, sliced

½ medium seedless cucumber,
    thinly sliced

In a large zip-top freezer bag, combine the soy sauce, vegetable oil, apple juice, and rub. Add the tuna steaks to the bag and refrigerate for at least 15 minutes but no longer than 2 hours.

Heat a charcoal grill (see page 4) or gas grill (see page 5) to medium-high heat.

Remove the tuna from the marinade and discard the marinade. Slide the tuna steaks onto the grill, close the grill, and cook the fish for about 5 minutes. If you like your tuna rare, take the fish off now. If you like it medium-well, flip the steaks and grill, closed, for about 5 minutes more, until the fish flakes easily with a fork.

In a small bowl, combine the mayonnaise and sauce; spread the mixture on the cut sides of the buns. Layer the lettuce, tuna, tomatoes, and cucumbers in each bun. Serve immediately.

Smoked Bacon BLTs

A BLT is so elemental and delicious that a good one is a like a gift from God, and I'm not even a religious man. When you make a BLT with bacon that's been properly smoked on the smoker, it becomes an even better experience. You want to get close to the angels without having to try too hard? Me, too. Eat this.

Makes 4 sandwiches

1 pound pork belly side
3 tablespoons Only Sauce (page 24)
3 tablespoons mayonnaise
8 thick slices rustic white bread, toasted and hot
16 tomato slices
8 leaves butter lettuce

Wash and thoroughly dry the pork belly. Place the pork belly in a large zip-top bag; pour the sauce over the top and massage it in. Seal the bag and refrigerate for at least 4 hours or, preferably, overnight.

When ready to cook, prepare a smoker with soaked wood chips and heat it to 150°F (see page 6). Alternatively, prepare a charcoal grill (see page 7) or gas grill (see page 8) for smoking and heat it to medium-low heat.

Prepare the pork belly: Use a sharp knife to score the pork belly by making a few slices going in both directions across it. Place the pork belly in a medium aluminum pan, place the pan in the smoker, cover, and let it smoke for 1 hour. Remove the pan from the smoker. Let the pork belly rest uncovered for 10 minutes. Using a sharp knife, thinly slice the pork belly.

To assemble the sandwiches: Spread the mayonnaise over the toasted bread. Top each with 4 tomato slices, a quarter of the pork belly, and 2 lettuce leaves. Serve immediately.

Barbecue Veggie Sandwiches

Yes, I have friends and neighbors and relatives who are vegetarians too. And in this day and age, when we are all so focused on healthy eating, even a pitmaster like me is looking to get more veggies into his diet. Here's a painless way to do just that. These sandwiches are great for a weekend lunch, when you're hanging out in the backyard and don't necessarily feel like working too hard. If you like, slip a piece of cheese on these sandwiches when the vegetables are just off the grill; I like the way pepper Jack pairs with the sauce. (Be sure to slice the veggies lengthwise to protect them from falling through the grill grate.)

Makes 4 sandwiches

2 teaspoons Only Other Rub (page 23)
1½ teaspoons red wine vinegar
¾ cup olive oil
1 eggplant, cut lengthwise into ½-inch slices
1 zucchini, cut lengthwise into ½-inch slices
2 bell peppers, cored, seeded, and cut lengthwise into wedges
1 red onion, cut into ½-inch slices
2 tablespoons mayonnaise
4 large crusty rolls, split
2 tablespoons Only Sauce (page 24)
4 leaves romaine lettuce
2 tomatoes, sliced

Heat a charcoal grill (see page 4) or gas grill (see page 5) to medium heat.

In a large bowl, combine the rub, vinegar, and olive oil. Add the eggplant, zucchini, bell peppers, and onions and toss to coat. Grill the vegetables in batches, turning once, until lightly browned and tender, 10 to 15 minutes per batch.

Spread 1 tablespoon of the mayonnaise over the cut side of the top of each roll. Spread the bottom of each roll with 1 tablespoon of the sauce. Sandwich the grilled vegetables, lettuce, and tomatoes in the rolls. Serve immediately.

four

SMOKED AND GRILLED

PERFECT APPLE-GLAZED BARBECUE PORK CHOPS

PERFECT GRILLED RIB EYES

BARBECUE FLANK STEAK

FORGET-ABOUT-IT EYE OF THE ROUND ROAST

SMOKY BARBECUE CHICKEN THIGHS & LEGS

MYRON'S DR PEPPER CAN CHICKEN

SMOKED TURKEY DRUMSTICKS

SMOKED MEATLOAF

GRILLED BALSAMIC CHICKEN BREASTS

GRILLED GINGER-PEACH CHICKEN BREASTS

GRILLED LEMON PEPPER WHOLE CHICKEN

GRILLED HAMBURGER STEAKS WITH ONIONS

APRICOT-GLAZED SLOW-SMOKED LEG OF LAMB

BARBECUE SWEET AND SOUR RACK OF LAMB

BARBECUE STEAK FAJITAS

SPAGHETTI AND SMOKED MEATBALLS

For me, the heart of barbecue is all about cooking meat, infusing it with smoke and other flavors to make it more delicious. This is a very simple concept, but it's become complicated in the eyes of a lot of home cooks. You've got a lot of people, so-called barbecue authorities even, telling you that if you don't marinate, inject, rub, and mop your meat according to precise specifications, you're doing it wrong. The idea of a "right" way is a big bunch of nonsense.

The truth is, I don't want folks getting in a tizzy over the cook times and temperatures so precisely that they can't enjoy themselves. Everyday good cooking's about keeping a level head, which you can achieve by staying calm and organized, and remembering that barbecuing is a simple art.

In this chapter I'm giving you dishes that fall into two categories: tried-and-true barbecue classics that you can do in faster and simpler ways (like my Perfect Grilled Rib Eyes, page 83), and other dishes I consider "new classics" that employ the usual barbecue cooking techniques but slightly updated to modern tastes (see my Apricot-Glazed Slow-Smoked Leg of Lamb, page 100).

So this is a "big meat" chapter, centered on how you can smoke or grill some really solid main courses on a busy weeknight or for friends and family, or both. I mean no disrespect to my fellow barbecue cookbook writers when I say that I'm not going to give you a book full of recipes that you can't use. I'm giving you real-deal actual recipes that I cook in my backyard for my own family. These aren't competition recipes; these are recipes people can use anytime.

There are a couple of things I'd like you to keep in mind when you're sorting out what you're cooking for dinner from this chapter full of delicious main courses. The first one is: Don't open your smoker if you don't have to. I realize that a lot of recipes instruct you to open your grill and flip something every other minute. My philosophy is different, and I'll tell you why: Every time you open your grill or smoker, you lower the temperature inside it by at least 5 degrees. And when you're barbecuing, it's important to maintain a consistent temperature. So if I tell you to flip something over, it's only because it's absolutely necessary.

If you're smoking, either in a smoker or a charcoal or gas grill, use the kind of wood you like. I like fruitwoods because they have a mild flavor and few impurities in them. I live in Georgia, and I have great access to peach wood. Use what you have easy access to, or use hickory or mesquite or whatever you like. This is your barbecue, your food. Don't know what kind of wood you like? Experiment until you figure it out—in that case, it's all about the journey, and with these recipes, you're going to have a great time getting there.

My goal for you is to have a handful of proven recipes in your repertoire, recipes that you can go to whenever it's time to make dinner, whatever the occasion (or lack thereof). You don't have to make it hard for yourself if you don't feel like it.

Perfect Apple-Glazed Barbecue Pork Chops

Think of this dish as the smoked version of pork chops and applesauce, that classic oven-roasted dish that we're fixing to make a whole lot better by cooking it over an open fire and turning the sauce into a finger-licking glaze.

Serves 8

1 quart plus ¼ cup apple juice
2 tablespoons light brown sugar
2 tablespoons extra-virgin olive oil
4 teaspoons Only Rub (page 22)
8 bone-in pork chops, about 1 inch thick (10 to 12 ounces each)
1 cup ketchup
6 garlic cloves, thinly sliced
¼ cup red wine vinegar
Salt

In each of 2 large resealable plastic bags, combine 2 tablespoons of the apple juice, 1 tablespoon of the brown sugar, 1 tablespoon of the olive oil, and 2 teaspoons of the rub. Seal the bags and shake to mix. Place 4 pork chops in each bag, seal, and shake again to coat the chops. Refrigerate for at least 4 hours or overnight.

Make the glaze: In a large saucepan, combine the remaining 1 quart apple juice with the ketchup, garlic, and vinegar and bring to a boil over high heat, stirring once or twice. Reduce the heat to medium and simmer, stirring occasionally, until reduced to 2 cups, about 30 minutes. Season with salt.

Heat a charcoal grill (see page 4) or gas grill (see page 5) to high heat.

Remove the pork chops from the marinade, discard the marinade, and season the chops with salt. Grill uncovered until nicely charred and just pink in the center, about 12 minutes per side. Brush a thick layer of the glaze on each chop, cover the grill, and

continued

cook until the pork is nicely bronzed, about 3 minutes. Remove from the grill, loosely cover with foil, and rest for 10 minutes before serving.

Make it in the oven: Marinate the pork chops and make the glaze as directed above. When ready to cook the pork chops, preheat the oven to 400°F. Remove the chops from the marinade, discard the marinade, and heat 2 tablespoons olive oil in a large ovenproof skillet over medium-high heat. Working in batches, cook the chops until browned, 3 to 5 minutes per side, transferring them to a plate when done. Arrange the chops in 1 large or 2 small roasting pans, brush a thick layer of the glaze on each chop, cover loosely with foil, and cook in the oven until the pork is cooked through, 8 to 11 minutes. Remove the pan from the oven and rest for 10 minutes before uncovering and serving.

Perfect Grilled Rib Eyes

The rib eye is a boneless, very tender, very flavorful cut of meat that comes from the animal's rib section; it's the same cut of meat as a prime rib, only with the rib removed. You want it to be thick, and you want it to be the best grade of meat you can afford (like "prime"). A rib eye is considered ideal for the grill; it's thick and juicy, and it has impeccable flavor. You don't need to do very much to it at all, except know how to grill.

Serves 8 to 16

Eight 1½- to 1¾-inch-thick large rib eye steaks, about 20 ounces each
2 tablespoons Only Rub (page 22)
¼ cup extra-virgin olive oil

Heat a charcoal grill (see page 4) or gas grill (see page 5) to high heat.

Season the steaks with the rub on both sides and work it in with your hands. Using your hands or a brush, evenly but lightly coat the steaks with the olive oil.

Place the steaks on the grate, decrease the heat to medium, close the lid, and do not move the steaks until they are well marked and have a light char, 4 to 5 minutes. Flip, close the lid, and continue to cook with the lid down to desired doneness: about 5 minutes per side for rare, about 6 minutes per side for medium-rare, about 7 minutes per side for medium, and 9 to 10 minutes per side for medium-well to well done.

Barbecue Flank Steak

Flank steak is the name given to the lean, boneless cut of meat that comes from the underside of the animal. It's thin and tough on its own, yes, but it's easy to tenderize with a marinade, and a quick cook time over high heat does wonders to bring out its natural meaty flavor. To cut a flank steak, you have to do it against the grain (otherwise it's too hard to chew). I like to have it for dinner in the summertime, especially served with corn on the cob and sliced tomatoes.

Serves 8 to 10

1½ tablespoons Only Rub (page 22)
3 tablespoons beer, preferably lager
2½ tablespoons Only Sauce (page 24)
2 teaspoons sugar
Three 1¼-pound flank steaks
Salt

In a small bowl, combine the rub, beer, sauce, and sugar.

Heat a charcoal grill (see page 4) or gas grill (see page 5) to medium-high heat.

Arrange the steaks on a baking sheet and rub them all over with the spice and beer mixture. Let stand for 10 minutes.

Season the flank steaks lightly with salt. Grill uncovered, turning once, until the steaks are medium-rare, about 8 minutes. Transfer the steaks from the grill to cutting boards (you'll probably need more than one) and let rest for 5 minutes. Slice the meat ¼ inch thick on a diagonal across the grain. Serve immediately.

Forget-About-It Eye of the Round Roast

The eye of the round is a cut from the cow's hind leg, and it's a long oval-shaped roast with very little fat on it. It's a big hunk of meat with a lot of connective tissue that needs to be broken down, so it's undervalued and often inexpensive. But a lot of savvy home cooks have known how to make the most of it. And you can make a truly delicious roast with eye of the round if you cook it using this technique, which starts off with very high heat and gradually lowers as the meat cooks through to break down the fat and connective tissue. What you end up with is an excellent roast of beef. The great thing here is that the temperature and timing do all the work; you don't even need to marinate this roast.

Serves 6

One 3-pound beef eye of the round roast
¼ cup Only Rub (page 22)

Prepare a smoker with soaked wood chips and heat it to 500°F (see page 6). Alternatively, prepare a charcoal grill (see page 7) or gas grill (see page 8) for smoking and heat it to high heat.

Season the roast all over with the rub. Place the roast, uncovered, in an aluminum roasting pan.

Place the roast in the smoker, cover, and immediately turn off the heat. Let the roast smoke for about 2 hours, until the internal temperature reaches 125 to 130°F for medium-rare. Do not open the smoker at all during this time. Remove from the smoker and let rest at room temperature for 15 to 20 minutes before carving (the meat temperature will rise 5 to 10 degrees after it is removed from the smoker), then thinly slice and serve.

Make it in the oven: Preheat the oven to 500°F. Place the roast in the oven, then immediately reduce the oven temperature to 475°F and roast for about 21 minutes. Turn

continued

off the oven and leave the roast undisturbed in the hot oven for 2½ hours. Do not open the door at all during this time. After 2½ hours open the oven door to check the temperature of the roast; it should have reached 145°F. (If it hasn't, let it cook for 10 minutes more, and recheck the temperature accordingly.) Let the roast rest, loosely covered, for 5 minutes, then thinly slice and serve.

Smoky Barbecue Chicken Thighs & Legs

I come in praise of chicken thighs: They're inexpensive, they're versatile (you can braise them, roast them, grill them, smoke them), and they've got enough fat to give them a boost of flavor. And the naturally richer flavor of dark meat is better for grilling than the blander, milder flavor of the breast. This is a straight-up easy recipe, maybe the easiest one in the book, and the best idea for dinner on a busy weeknight that I've had in ages. I prefer bone-in thighs myself, but you can use boneless, which cook faster and are neater to eat.

Serves 6 to 8

8 whole chicken legs, split, or 8 drumsticks and 8 thighs (about 5 pounds total)
½ cup Only Other Rub (page 23)
Only Sauce (page 24) for serving, optional

Heat a charcoal grill (see page 10) or gas grill (see page 8) set up for indirect heat to medium-high heat.

Wash the chicken pieces thoroughly and pat them dry with paper towels. Apply the rub all over the exposed areas of the chicken pieces.

Arrange the chicken on the hot grate above the drip pan and away from the coals or burner, skin side down. Cover and grill for 40 minutes, or until the skin is crisp and the meat is cooked through. Transfer to plates and serve with sauce if you like.

Myron's Dr Pepper Can Chicken

You've heard of beer can chicken, right? You stick a can of beer in a chicken cavity, put it on the grill, and it steams while it roasts. Simple, yes, but it's still a fairly ingenious way to cook a chicken. The liquid inside the cavity keeps the meat moist while the smoky flavor permeates from the outside. The thing is, it's better with Dr Pepper. Why? Because Dr Pepper has more sugar in it, and the sweet flavor goes even better with the smoke. And then you can save your beer and drink it while you're cooking.

Serves 4

¼ cup plus 2 tablespoons Only Other Rub (page 23)
One 3- to 4-pound whole chicken
½ cup (1 stick) unsalted butter
One 12-ounce can Dr Pepper, halfway full
Only Sauce (page 24) for serving, optional

Apply ¼ cup of the rub under and on the skin of the chicken. Let the chicken rest in the refrigerator for 1 hour.

While the chicken is resting, heat a charcoal grill (see page 10) or gas grill (see page 8) set up for indirect heat to medium heat. Alternatively, prepare a smoker with soaked wood chips and heat it to 275°F (see page 6).

Melt the butter in a small saucepan over low heat. Stir in the remaining 2 tablespoons rub until dissolved and remove from the heat. Baste the chicken with the seasoned butter. Stand the chicken on the open can so that the can is inside the cavity. Stand upright on the grill.

Grill, covered, over indirect heat, until an instant-read thermometer inserted into the thickest part of the thigh reads 175°F, about 3 hours. To maintain the temperature at 275°F, replenish the charcoal with a fresh batch of burning coals every hour and add more water to the drip pan when half of it is evaporated.

Remove and discard the can. Transfer the bird to a carving board and let rest for 20 minutes before serving. Serve with sauce on the side if you like.

Smoked Turkey Drumsticks

Ever been to a BBQ competition or state fair and seen people waving around those giant bronzed turkey legs, big and meaty and juicy? You can make them in your own backyard, and you won't have to contend with the crowds. The cure helps keep the legs juicy by locking in the moisture. But keep in mind that turkey legs have a lot of connective tissue, which needs to be broken down with high heat.

Makes 4 large drumsticks

½ gallon water

½ cup kosher salt

¼ cup dark brown sugar

1 teaspoon ground allspice

1 teaspoon ground coriander

1 teaspoon dry mustard

4 turkey drumsticks

2 tablespoons olive oil

2 tablespoons Only Other Rub (page 23)

Cure the legs: In a large bowl, combine the water, salt, sugar, allspice, coriander, and mustard; stir to dissolve the seasonings. Pour the curing solution into a large zip-top bag and add the turkey legs. Place the bag in a large aluminum baking pan and refrigerate for 24 hours.

When ready to smoke, prepare a charcoal grill (see page 7) or gas grill (see page 8) with soaked wood chips and heat it to 250°F. Alternatively, prepare a smoker with soaked wood chips (see page 6) and heat it to 250°F, or preheat the oven to 275°F.

Remove the turkey legs from the curing liquid and rinse off in cold water. Pat the legs dry with paper towels. Coat the legs with the olive oil, then, using your fingers, lightly coat them with the rub.

Grill (covered), smoke (covered), or roast (covered) in the oven on a roasting pan for about 3 hours, until the temperature of the legs reads 180°F on an instant-read thermometer. To crisp the skin on the smoker, leave the drumsticks on for 15 additional minutes after the internal temperature has reached 180°F. In the oven or on the gas grill, turn the heat up to 350 or 400°F and cook, covered, watching carefully to make sure the skin does not burn, for about 10 additional minutes.

Pull the legs out and wrap each in foil to rest. Remove the foil and serve immediately.

Smoked Meatloaf

I'm a man who loves meatloaf. And what's even better than oven-roasted meatloaf? Meatloaf that's kissed by smoke, that you can throw on the grill or smoker and infuse with that essence of outdoor cooking. This ain't your grandmama's meatloaf, and believe me when I tell you it's better.

Makes one 9-inch meatloaf; serves about 6

½ cup milk
1 cup Only Sauce (page 24), plus ¼ cup for basting
1 cup finely crushed Ritz crackers (about 20 crackers)
2 pounds 80% lean ground beef
¼ teaspoon ground nutmeg, or to taste
½ cup grated Parmigiano-Reggiano cheese
1 large egg, beaten
1 tablespoon Only Rub (page 22)
Salt and freshly ground black pepper

Prepare a charcoal grill (see page 7) or gas grill (see page 8) for smoking with soaked wood chips set up for indirect heat, and heat it to medium heat. Alternatively, prepare a smoker with soaked wood chips and heat it to 350°F (see page 6).

In a large bowl, whisk together the milk and 1 cup of the sauce. Stir in the crackers, ground beef, nutmeg, cheese, and egg and mix well. Pack the mixture into a 9 x 5-inch loaf pan or 10 x 6-inch baking dish.

When the grill is ready, place the meatloaf pan on the cool side of the grill. Cover the grill and smoke the meatloaf as close to 200°F as possible until the interior temperature of the meatloaf registers 140°F on an instant-read thermometer. At that point, brush the remaining ¼ cup sauce on top of the meatloaf and cover the grill. The glaze will set while the meatloaf reaches its final temperature of 150 to 160°F. The total cooking time will depend on the heat of your fire and the size of your baking pan or dish, but expect about 3 hours. Transfer the meatloaf pan to a heatproof surface, cover it with aluminum foil, and allow it to rest for 20 minutes before slicing and serving.

Make it in the oven: Preheat the oven to 375°F and prepare the meatloaf as directed above. Bake for 1 hour and 10 minutes, or until the glaze is browned and an instant-read thermometer inserted in the center of the meatloaf reads 150 to 160°F. Remove the meatloaf from the oven, season to taste with Only Rub, salt, and pepper, and let it rest, loosely covered, for 10 minutes before slicing and serving.

Grilled Balsamic Chicken Breasts

There are two things you need to think about when you're grilling chicken breasts, which we all like to do because they're a nice low-fat protein that's quick to cook. The first is flavor: White meat chicken is mild, so you need to pair it with a strong flavor. (In this recipe, the balsamic vinegar does the trick.) The second issue is how to keep it from getting dried out, which is the number one problem with cooking chicken on a grill. We're going to combat that by keeping the skin on the breast and thus insulating the meat and keeping it juicy (I eat the crisp skin, but you can always peel it off after you're cooking if you're opposed to it) and by marinating the chicken before I cook it to seal in the juices.

Serves 4

4 chicken breast halves on the bone with skin (about 2 pounds)
½ cup chicken stock
1 cup balsamic vinegar
1½ tablespoons Worcestershire sauce
2 tablespoons minced garlic
2 teaspoons dry mustard
1 teaspoon freshly ground black pepper
2 tablespoons sugar
¼ cup Dijon mustard

Rinse the chicken breasts thoroughly and pat them dry. Place them in a gallon-size zip-top bag.

Combine the remaining ingredients in a medium bowl and pour the marinade over the chicken. Seal the bag and refrigerate for at least 4 and up to 24 hours, turning occasionally.

When ready to cook, heat a charcoal grill (see page 10) or gas grill (see page 8) set up for indirect heat to high heat.

Place the chicken on the grill skin side up. Cover and grill the chicken until browned and just cooked through, about 30 minutes. Turn the breasts over and grill until the skin is crisp and lightly charred, about 2 minutes longer. Let the breasts rest, covered, for 5 minutes, then serve immediately.

Make it in the oven: Marinate the chicken breasts as directed above, but do not discard the marinade. When ready to cook, preheat the oven to 400°F. Pat the chicken breasts dry with a clean paper towel. Arrange the chicken skin side up in a 13 by 9-inch baking dish. Pour the marinade over the chicken and bake for 20 minutes, then baste the chicken thoroughly with the pan juices. Bake for about 20 minutes more, until the juices of the breasts run clear with no tinge of pink when pricked with a fork. Serve the breasts hot with juices poured over them if you like.

Grilled Ginger-Peach Chicken Breasts

Ginger and peach form a great flavor combination. If you haven't tried them together, you need to. Especially here, where the ginger-peach flavors are enhanced by the element of smoke cooking it on the grill imparts.

Serves 4

½ cup peach preserves, large pieces snipped
1 tablespoon white wine vinegar
1 tablespoon prepared horseradish
1 tablespoon grated fresh ginger or 1 teaspoon dried ginger
½ teaspoon salt
½ teaspoon coarsely ground black pepper
4 chicken breast halves on the bone with skin (about 2 pounds)

In a small microwave-safe bowl, combine the preserves, vinegar, horseradish, ginger, salt, and pepper. Microwave, uncovered, on 100% power (high) for 30 to 60 seconds, until the preserves are melted, stirring once halfway through the cooking time. Set aside to cool.

Rinse the chicken pieces thoroughly and pat them dry. Place the chicken in a gallon-size zip-top bag and pour the cooled marinade over the chicken. Seal the bag and refrigerate for at least 6 and up to 24 hours, turning occasionally.

When ready to cook, heat a charcoal grill (see page 10) or gas grill (see page 8) set up for indirect heat to high heat.

Place the chicken on the grill skin side up. Cover and grill the chicken until browned and just cooked through, about 30 minutes. Turn the breasts over, cover, and grill until the skin is crisp and lightly charred, about 2 minutes longer. Let the breasts rest, covered, for 5 minutes, then serve immediately.

Make it in the oven: Marinate the chicken breasts as directed above, but do not discard the marinade. When ready to cook, preheat the oven to 400°F. Pat the chicken breasts dry with a clean paper towel. Arrange the chicken breasts skin side up in a 13 by 9-inch baking dish. Pour the marinade over the chicken and bake for 20 minutes, then baste the chicken thoroughly with the pan juices. Bake for about 20 minutes more, until the juices of the breasts run clear with no tinge of pink when pricked with a fork. Serve the breasts hot with juices poured over them if you like.

Grilled Lemon Pepper Whole Chicken

Lemon-pepper chicken is another one of those time-honored combinations known to home cooks everywhere because it's so basic and delicious. It's also extremely easy to create by combining store-bought lemon curd with a little fresh lemon juice and covering a whole chicken with it. The thick curd combined with the bite of the pepper gives the bird added succulence.

Serves 4

2 tablespoons extra-virgin olive oil
1 tablespoon minced garlic
½ cup prepared lemon curd
2 tablespoons fresh lemon juice
1 teaspoon Louisiana-style hot sauce
3 tablespoons coarsely ground black pepper
One 4-pound chicken, rinsed and patted dry

Heat the olive oil in a small saucepan over medium heat. Add the garlic and cook until fragrant, about 1 minute. Whisk in the lemon curd, lemon juice, and ¼ cup water and bring to a boil. Immediately remove from the heat. Whisk in the hot sauce and pepper and cool to room temperature. Spread half of the mixture under the chicken's skin and rub the remaining mixture all over the skin. Tie the chicken's legs together with kitchen string.

Heat a charcoal grill (see page 10) or gas grill (see page 8) set up for indirect heat, and heat it to medium-high heat.

Set the chicken on the grill, breast side up, over the drip pan, away from the heat. Cover and grill until the skin is crisp and an instant-read thermometer inserted into the inner thigh registers 165°F, about 1½ hours. Transfer to a cutting board and let stand for 10 minutes, loosely covered, then cut the chicken into pieces and serve.

Make it in the oven: Prepare the chicken. Preheat the oven to 425°F. Place the chicken in an aluminum pan and roast for about 1 hour, until the juices run clear when an inner thigh is pierced. Transfer the chicken to a carving board, loosely cover, and let rest for 10 minutes, then cut the chicken into pieces and serve.

Grilled Hamburger Steaks with Onions

If you grew up like I did eating hamburger steaks with gravy and mashed potatoes, then I don't need to explain to you why this recipe isn't in the Burgers chapter. This is a thick patty meant to be eaten with a knife and fork. When you make it outdoors, you can top the patties with sweet grilled onion "relish" instead of the gravy. This here is what you call a good old-fashioned supper.

Serves 2 to 4

1 pound 80% lean ground beef

2 tablespoons steak sauce

One 1-ounce envelope onion soup mix

Cooking spray

2 large Bermuda or other sweet onions, cut in half, then thinly sliced and separated
   (about 6 cups)

2 tablespoons packed dark brown sugar

1 tablespoon balsamic vinegar

Heat a charcoal grill (see page 4) or gas grill (see page 5) to medium heat.

Gently shape the ground beef into 4 thin patties, each about ½ inch thick. Take care not to overhandle the meat.

Brush the beef patties with the steak sauce and sprinkle with half of the dry soup mix.

Spray two 18 x 12-inch sheets of heavy-duty foil with cooking spray. Place half of the onions on the center of each foil piece. Sprinkle with the remaining soup mix, the brown sugar, and the vinegar. Fold the foil over the onions so the edges meet. Seal the edges, making a tight ½-inch fold; fold again. Allow some space on the sides for circulation and expansion.

Cover and grill the onion packets and beef patties for 10 to 15 minutes, turning the patties and rotating the packets a half turn once or twice, until an instant-read thermometer inserted in the center of a patty reads 160°F. Place the packets and patties on plates. Cut a large X across the top of each packet, fold back the foil, and serve.

Apricot-Glazed Slow-Smoked Leg of Lamb

We don't have a lot of lamb in South Georgia, where we traditionally eat a whole lot of pork, but I sure like its gamy flavor (and besides, I had to figure out how to cook lamb if I wanted to win money in some mutton-cooking professional barbecue contests, which I did). The Mediterranean-inspired flavor combo of lamb and apricots is very appealing, but you know I had to make it a barbecue pitmaster's version. (A note about cooking leg of lamb: The "aitchbone" is the split portion of an animal's pelvic bone; it is located on the leg/rump cuts and is generally wishbone shaped. It's often removed for more even and consistent cooking and, especially, more even carving and serving. Do you have to remove it? Nope. But if you have a butcher you like, it's easy enough to ask to have this done, and even have him tie it up for you. If not, it's not going to be a problem.)

Serves 8

½ cup Only Rub (page 22)
One 7- to 7½-pound leg of lamb, trimmed of any excess fat and sinew
1 cup apple juice
4 tablespoons (½ stick) unsalted butter
¼ cup apricot jelly

Apply the rub all over the meat. Wrap with plastic wrap and refrigerate for at least 3 hours or, preferably, overnight.

Prepare a smoker with soaked wood chips and heat it to 250°F (see page 6). Alternatively, prepare a charcoal grill (see page 7) or gas grill (see page 8) for smoking and heat it to medium heat.

Unwrap the meat from the plastic and place it on the grill. Cover and grill for 4 hours, opening the smoker only to spritz the meat with apple juice every hour after the first hour.

continued on page 102

Remove the lamb from the grill. Transfer the lamb to the center of a large piece of heavy-duty aluminum foil and securely wrap it. Place back on the grill, cover, and cook for about 1 hour more.

Remove the lamb from the grill. Let rest, still wrapped, for 30 minutes.

Meanwhile, melt the butter in a small saucepan over low heat. Stir in the apricot jelly until dissolved and remove from the heat.

Carefully unwrap the lamb and brush the apricot jelly mixture over the entire surface. Place the lamb back on the grill, cover, and cook for 30 minutes to set the glaze. Remove the lamb from the grill to a carving board and let rest, loosely covered, for 10 to 15 minutes, then slice the lamb against the grain and serve.

Make it in the oven: Prepare the lamb as directed above. When ready to cook, preheat the oven to 400°F, place the lamb in a roasting pan, and roast for 30 minutes. Reduce the oven temperature to 350°F and continue roasting 1 hour longer, or until an instant-read thermometer inserted into the thickest part of the leg reads 145°F. Remove the lamb from the oven and let rest, loosely covered, for 10 to 15 minutes.

Meanwhile, melt the butter in a small saucepan over low heat. Stir in the apricot jelly until dissolved and remove from the heat.

Carefully unwrap the lamb and brush the apricot jelly mixture over the entire surface. Place the lamb back in the oven, cover, and cook for 30 minutes to set the glaze. Remove the lamb from the oven to a carving board and let rest, loosely covered, for 10 to 15 minutes, then slice the lamb against the grain and serve.

HOW TO FRENCH A RACK OF LAMB

To "French" the lamb is a classic way of preparing rack of lamb, leaving each chop with the first few inches of fat removed from the bones. It gives the rack a cleaner look. These days you can usually find packaged lamb racks already Frenched, or if you have access to a butcher, he or she should be able to prepare it for you. But you can do it yourself too, following these instructions.

Stand the lamb rack up on one end so that you can see the "eye" of the lamb chop. Score the fat side at the edge about an inch and a half or so up the rib from the eye to use as a cutting guideline. Do the same on the other end of the rack. Using a sharp knife, cut through the fatty side of the rib roast, to the bone, from one marked end to the other. Then go back over your cut and, holding the knife perpendicular to the roast, jab it in several places to go all the way through the other side, so that the reverse site gets "marked" with scores. Turn the rib rack over so that it is now bone side up. You should be able to see the markings made from the knife that got inserted from the other side. Those markings will delineate the boundary beyond which you will not cut. Working from the skinny ends of the rib bone, make a cut down along the bone, until you get to the previously scored marking, then cut across to the next rib and cut up to the end of that rib bone. Continue to do this until all of the bones have had the flesh cut around them. Turn the rack over again so that the fat side is on top, and begin to pull off the fat and flesh from the bones. Use your knife to help cut away any flesh that is sticking to the bones. Scrape away any residual flesh on the exposed bones. Use a towel to wipe the bones clean. Now your rack of lamb is perfectly "Frenched."

Barbecue Sweet and Sour Rack of Lamb

I like chops because I like foods that people can pick up and hold, like pizza and ribs and those giant turkey legs they serve at some barbecue competitions, state fairs, and the like. When I cook lamb chops I look for the largest rack I can find, so I've got chops I can easily handle and sink my teeth into. The sweet-and-sour glaze complements the lamb's natural flavor.

Serves 8

Four 1- to 1½-pound racks of lamb (each rack should have 8 ribs), trimmed of all but ¼-inch layer of fat and Frenched (see Box, page 103)
2 cups cranberry juice
½ cup soy sauce
2 tablespoons distilled white vinegar
1 tablespoon salt
2 tablespoons sugar
½ cup Only Rub (page 22)
1 cup Only Sauce (page 24)

Pat the racks of lamb dry with paper towels.

In a large aluminum baking pan, combine the cranberry juice, soy sauce, vinegar, salt, and sugar. Submerge the racks of lamb in the mixture, cover, and marinate in the refrigerator for at least 2 hours or, preferably, overnight.

When you are ready to cook, prepare a smoker with soaked wood chips and heat it to 325°F (see page 6). Alternatively, prepare a charcoal grill (see page 7) or gas grill (see page 8) for smoking and heat it to medium heat.

Remove the lamb from the marinade and discard the marinade. Season each rack lightly with the rub. Place the racks in a clean aluminum baking pan, place the pan in the smoker, cover, and cook for 25 minutes.

Remove the pan from the smoker and brush the racks with the sauce to glaze them. Put the pan back into the smoker, cover, and cook for about 5 additional minutes. Transfer the racks to a carving board and let rest, loosely covered, for 10 to 15 minutes, then slice between the ribs to separate the chops for serving.

Make it in the oven: Marinate the lamb as directed above, then season it with the rub. When you are ready to cook the lamb, preheat the oven to 425°F. Heat 1 large or 2 small roasting pans in the oven for about 10 minutes to thoroughly warm them. Using paper towels, pat the racks of lamb dry and coat lightly with 1 to 2 teaspoons of olive oil for each rack. Place the racks flesh side down in the pan or pans. Roast for 15 to 20 minutes, until an instant-read thermometer inserted into the thickest part of the rack reads 145°F. Remove the pan or pans from the oven and brush the racks with the sauce to glaze them. Put the pan or pans back into the oven, cover, and cook for 5 additional minutes. Transfer the racks to a carving board and let rest, loosely covered, for 10 to 15 minutes, then slice between the ribs to separate the chops for serving.

Barbecue Steak Fajitas

At my home in middle Georgia it actually takes less time to grill my own fajitas than it does to drive to the nearest Mexican restaurant, order them, and wait to be served. Fajitas are great for feeding a small group because everyone can fill them how they like, and the cook doesn't have to do much more than prepare the meat. A lot of cooks like to do this with flank steak, but I prefer slices of the more tender sirloin in my tortillas.

Serves 4

1 pound boneless beef sirloin steak, cut into thin strips
3 medium bell peppers, cored, seeded, and cut into ½-inch strips
1 medium onion, thinly sliced
1 tablespoon Only Rub (page 22)
⅓ cup chicken stock or water
8 medium flour tortillas
¾ cup salsa for serving, optional
¾ cup sour cream for serving, optional
1 cup grated sharp cheddar cheese for serving, optional

Heat a charcoal grill (see page 4) or gas grill (see page 5) to low heat.

Cut 4 large sheets of aluminum foil. In a large bowl, combine the beef strips, bell pepper strips, onion slices, rub, and stock.

Place one quarter of the beef mixture on the center of each foil sheet. Bring up 2 sides of the foil over the beef mixture so the edges meet. Seal the edges, making a tight ½-inch fold; fold again, allowing space for heat circulation. Fold the other sides to seal.

Place the packets on the grill, cover, and cook until the beef is done and the bell peppers and onions are tender, 13 to 18 minutes, depending on how you like your steak cooked.

To serve, cut a large X across the top of each packet; carefully fold back the foil to allow steam to escape. Serve the beef with tortillas and salsa, sour cream, and cheese if you like.

Spaghetti and Smoked Meatballs

Spaghetti and meatballs is one of my favorite dinners, only my idea of meatballs is something that comes off the grill. Smoky meatballs add a wonderful flavor to your marinara sauce. The secret to good light meatballs is often to add more bread (in this case, I like crumbled Ritz crackers) than most people are used to. But remember that meatballs were originally "poor people food"—just like barbecue—with the idea originally involving stretching the expensive ingredient, meat.

Serves 6

1 pound 80% lean ground beef
1 pound ground pork
½ sleeve Ritz crackers, crushed (about ¾ cup)
1 egg, beaten
¼ cup ketchup
2 slices white bread, lightly moistened with water and torn into small pieces
1 medium onion, chopped
Salt and freshly ground black pepper
One 28-ounce can pureed tomatoes
1 pound dried spaghetti
Grated Parmesan cheese for serving, optional

Prepare a smoker with soaked wood chips and heat it to 350°F (see page 6). Alternatively, prepare a charcoal grill (see page 7) or gas grill (see page 8) for smoking and heat it to medium-high heat.

In a large bowl, using your hands, thoroughly combine the beef, pork, crushed crackers, egg, ketchup, bread pieces, and onions, and season with salt and pepper. Form the mixture into 24 smallish meatballs, each about the size of a tablespoon.

Place the meatballs in a large aluminum baking pan and cover with the pureed tomatoes. Cover the meatballs and place the pan on the grill. Smoke until the meatballs are cooked through and the center of one registers 140°F on an instant-read thermometer, about 45 minutes. Remove the pan from the smoker and set aside to rest.

Meanwhile, bring a large pot of salted water to boil; cook the spaghetti to al dente according to the package directions. Drain and return the pasta to the pot. Pour in about 1 cup of the tomato sauce from the baking pan and toss until the pasta is well coated, about 1 minute. Transfer the pasta to large, shallow bowls and spoon the meatballs and remaining tomato sauce over the spaghetti. Serve immediately, passing grated cheese at the table if you like.

five

BARBECUE-FRIED

BARBECUE-FRIED BABY BACKS

BARBECUE-FRIED CHICKEN LOLLIPOPS

BUTTERMILK FRIED BARBECUE CHICKEN

BARBECUE-FRIED CATFISH ON A STICK

BARBECUE-FRIED PORK TENDERLOIN SANDWICHES

BARBECUE-FRIED CAP'N CRUNCH CHICKEN TENDERS

Where I'm from if you're not barbecuing something, you're most likely frying it. That, in a sentence, is why Southern food is so good.

Yes: My two favorite kinds of cooking are barbecuing and frying. So I have always wondered: Why aren't there any foods that are barbecued and fried? What a beautiful combination that would be, I used to think. And then I started getting serious about the concept.

I want you to embrace this with me: I'm not going to apologize for the fact that barbecue-fried foods are decadent, over the top, and better than just about anything else you can enjoy with your clothes on.

And yes, I do realize that in general fried foods are not considered "good for you." So I'm going to tell you that this chapter is about one thing: having fun in the kitchen.

Because even I, the meanest, most low-down competitor on the professional barbecue circuit, a man who would just as easily beat the pants off you in a contest as he would say howdy, yes, even I like to have fun in the kitchen.

And one of the most fun things to do that I could think of in a long, long time was to figure out how to make some dishes that were both barbecued *and* fried.

So if you're worried about fat and calories and dying an early death because you didn't spend your whole life eating nothing but kale and flaxseed, let me tell you something: For a barbecue cookbook, this one is packed with healthy side dishes and protein preparations that will feed your brains and bodies just perfectly. This here chapter, however, is full of treats—special-occasion foods meant to wow your guests. Dishes with ingenuity and charm (I thought of them, didn't I?) because they're combining two excellent techniques. You might love my slow-smoked tomatoes, and they're damn good, but it's my barbecue-fried chicken lollipops that are going to make their way into your dreams.

So, once more, with feeling: Have some fun. Barbecue-fry yourself up a stick of catfish and pop a cold Stella and chill out every once in a while. You got to manage your stress if you want to live forever, ya know.

Barbecue-Fried Baby Backs

One day I was eating a rib—my favorite kind of rib, the baby back—and I was thinking, damn, this is good, but wouldn't it be better if it was also a little crunchy? Rather than having you smoke racks of ribs and *then* fry them, which would take you damn near forever, I'm going to have you braise these ribs in the oven until they're moist and tender, which is far less laborious, and then you can save your energy for the last-minute frying. Warning: These ribs are so addictive, with their softly braised insides and crispy-salty crusts, that you may give up the smoked kind altogether.

Serves 4

4 cups Only Sauce (page 24)
1 cup ginger ale
3 tablespoons Only Rub (page 22)
3 racks of baby back ribs, about 2½ pounds
Peanut oil for frying
½ cup all-purpose flour
½ cup cornstarch

Preheat the oven to 400°F. In a large, heavy roasting pan, combine 2 cups of Only Sauce, ginger ale, and 2 tablespoons of the rub and stir together to combine. Set the pan over 2 burners and bring to a boil over medium-high heat.

Add the baby back ribs to the roasting pan, cover tightly with foil, transfer to the oven, and bake for about 2 hours, until the ribs are very tender when touched with a fork. Remove the pan from the oven, discard the liquid, and let the ribs cool to room temperature. Spread the ribs out in a single layer on a baking sheet and refrigerate until they are chilled and firm, about 30 minutes.

Meanwhile, heat the remaining 2 cups of Only Sauce in a large saucepan over medium-high heat for about 3 minutes to thoroughly warm through, stirring occasionally. Transfer the warm sauce to a large bowl and set aside.

In a large, sturdy pot, heat 1½ inches of peanut oil over medium heat to 375°F.

In a large bowl, whisk the flour with the cornstarch and the remaining 1 tablespoon rub and pour the mixture into a large zip-top bag. Cut the racks into individual ribs. Toss the ribs a few at a time into the bag with the flour and coat them, shaking off the excess as you remove them. Working in batches, fry the ribs until the coating is lightly golden and crisp, about 2 minutes per rib.

Transfer the ribs to paper towels to drain briefly, then dredge them through the sauce in the bowl, tossing to coat. Pile the ribs on a platter and serve immediately.

Barbecue-Fried Chicken Lollipops

I got the idea for barbecue chicken pieces that you can fry one day when I was working on recipes for my world-famous Cupcake Chicken. That's a very involved recipe with the time-consuming task of trimming up chicken thighs and several other steps. Much easier: You make these "lollipops" by taking drumettes and performing a process called Frenching to them. To French the drumettes, remove the excess fat from the bottom of each drumette by running a sharp knife along its base and peeling off the excess connective tissue and skin: That's all it takes to give these mini drumsticks the appearance of lollipops.

Serves 6 to 8 as an appetizer or snack

2 tablespoons Only Sauce (page 24), plus more for serving
2 tablespoons apple juice
½ cup all-purpose flour
¼ cup cornstarch
1 tablespoon Only Rub (page 22)
1 large egg, lightly beaten
Kosher salt
2 pounds chicken wing drumettes, meat pulled to one end, opposite end trimmed
Peanut oil for frying

In a large bowl, combine the sauce and apple juice. Stir in the flour, cornstarch, rub, egg, and salt to taste; add the chicken drumettes and toss to coat evenly with the marinade. Cover with plastic wrap and let sit at room temperature for 1 hour, or refrigerate for up to 4 hours.

Pour oil to a depth of 2 inches into a large, heavy-bottomed skillet such as cast iron, and heat over medium-high heat until a deep-fry thermometer reads 350°F. Working in batches, fry the chicken lollipops until golden brown and cooked through, about 7 minutes. Using a slotted spoon, transfer to paper towels to drain briefly before serving. Serve with more sauce for dipping if you like.

Buttermilk Fried Barbecue Chicken

I've said it before and I'll say it again: A good Southern cook has *got* to know how to fry chicken. I like small fresh chickens (as opposed to large previously frozen ones) for frying simply because the flavor of their meat is so much better, with a gentle sweetness. I like to fry chicken in pure pork lard, which is richer than anything out there; you can buy lard from a butcher (but don't buy the pre-packed kinds in supermarkets). If that's not your thing, peanut oil is an excellent substitute.

Serves 4

2 cups all-purpose flour
3 tablespoons Only Rub (page 22), plus more for sprinkling
2 large eggs
2 cups buttermilk
2 cups Only Sauce (page 24), plus more for dipping
1 small chicken, about 3 pounds, cut into 8 pieces (2 legs, 2 thighs, 2 breasts,
    2 wings)
1 to 1½ cups freshly rendered pork lard, of if you can't get that, peanut oil

In a large bowl, combine the flour with the rub. In another large bowl, beat the eggs with the buttermilk and sauce until well combined. Create a double layer of batter with each piece of chicken: Coat the chicken pieces in the egg-buttermilk-sauce mixture, then dredge them in the seasoned flour. Repeat the process, coating the chicken again with the egg-buttermilk-sauce mixture and then dredging it again in the seasoned flour mixture. Set the coated pieces on a clean platter or baking sheet.

Pour the lard or oil to a depth of about 1 inch in a large cast-iron skillet and heat it over medium heat until the temperature reaches 325°F on a deep-fry thermometer. Add the chicken pieces in batches and fry for about 20 minutes, turning them over halfway through the cooking. The wings will be done after about 10 minutes, so remove them early. Drain the chicken thoroughly on paper towels, sprinkle additional rub on the pieces, and serve immediately, with extra sauce on the side for dipping if you like.

Barbecue-Fried Catfish on a Stick

These snacks are a bit like corndogs in that they're deep-fried and on a stick, only they're made with fish and are coated with barbecue sauce in their batter. OK, so maybe they're not like corndogs. What they are is very easy to make, and a perfect appetizer for when you're waiting for a big piece of meat to rest after it comes out of the smoker but before it's ready to eat. When you're ready to cook these, they fry up fast, and before you know it they're gone.

Note: If you are using wooden skewers, soak them in water for 30 minutes before using to prevent them from burning on the grill.

Serves 6 as an appetizer (2 skewers per person)

4 catfish fillets (about 4 ounces each)
2 tablespoons Only Rub (page 22)
2 tablespoons Only Sauce (page 24), plus more for dipping
1 cup buttermilk
2 cups all-purpose flour
4 cups vegetable oil

Cut each fillet lengthwise into 3 strips, each about 1½ inches wide. Thread each strip onto a metal or wooden 10-inch skewer and lay them in a shallow bowl.

In a medium bowl, combine 1 tablespoon of the rub with the sauce and buttermilk; stir to blend thoroughly. Pour the mixture over the catfish, cover, and refrigerate for at least 4 hours or, preferably, overnight.

Remove the fish from the refrigerator. Heat the oil to 360°F in a large, deep cast-iron skillet over medium-high heat.

In a large bowl, combine the flour and the remaining 1 tablespoon rub. Dredge 2 to 3 skewers at a time in the flour, shaking off any excess. Fry the skewers in batches until the catfish "sticks" become golden brown, about 4 minutes on each side. Drain on paper towels. Serve the sticks hot with sauce on the side for dipping if you like.

Barbecue-Fried Pork Tenderloin Sandwiches

I heard about a "delicacy" served at the Iowa State Fair that sounded right up my alley: fried pork medallion sandwiches. I have a close, some might say intimate, relationship with cooking pork, but Iowa's the number one pork-producing state in the nation, so I figured I'd better try to figure out what they're doing. Turns out at the fair they pound out slices of pork tenderloin, fry them up, and put them on a bun. But I knew just how to make them better: Dredge them in some good old-fashioned hickory sauce before slapping them on a bun. Thank you, good people of Iowa.

Makes 6 to 8 sandwiches

1 to 2 pork tenderloins, about 2½ pounds total
3 tablespoons Only Rub (page 22)
1 cup all-purpose flour
Peanut oil for frying
1 cup Only Sauce (page 24)
Salt and freshly ground black pepper
8 hamburger buns, split
Mayonnaise and your favorite toppings, such as lettuce, tomato, and pickles

Cut the pork tenderloins into 1-inch medallions. Place the medallions between 2 pieces of plastic wrap or inside a zip-top bag, then pound them flat with a meat mallet or a heavy-bottomed skillet. Lay the medallions out on a large baking sheet or two and, using 2 tablespoons of the rub, season each medallion with rub on both sides.

In a large zip-top bag, combine the flour with the remaining 1 tablespoon rub. Shake each medallion in the flour mixture and stack them on a platter.

In a large, heavy-bottomed skillet such as cast iron, heat 1½ inches of peanut oil over medium heat to 375°F. Fry the medallions in batches, flipping each piece as soon as it begins to brown and curl at the edges; it will take just about 2 minutes total until one of these medallions is cooked on both sides.

Preheat the oven to 200°F.

In a medium, shallow saucepan, warm the sauce over medium heat, 3 to 5 minutes. Dredge each medallion through the sauce on both sides, transfer to a baking sheet, and repeat the process, transferring each sauce-coated medallion to the baking sheet in the oven to keep warm, until all medallions are finished.

To make the sandwiches, slather both cut sides of each hamburger bun with mayonnaise, layer on a barbecue-fried pork medallion or two, and top with your favorite toppings: I like a slice of lettuce, a slice of tomato, and a few bread-and-butter pickles.

Barbecue-Fried Cap'n Crunch Chicken Tenders

Coating chicken in cornflakes is not anything new in my part of the world. In fact, cornflake breading has become so common that it has almost transitioned into a traditional method. Now people have started "breading" chicken with almost everything, from ground-up dried soybeans to cinnamon graham crackers. My favorite of these is Cap'n Crunch cereal, which is sweet and addictive, a perfect foil for my hickory-enhanced barbecue sauce.

Serves 4 to 6 as an appetizer

2½ cups Cap'n Crunch cereal
1 cup corn flakes
1 large egg
½ cup Only Sauce (page 24), plus more for dipping
2 pounds boneless skinless chicken breast tenders
Vegetable oil for frying

In a large zip-top bag, combine the 2 cereals. Using a rolling pin, finely crush the cereals by rolling back and forth over the flattened bag until the cereals resemble colorful flour.

In a medium bowl, beat the egg with the sauce and set aside.

Dip the chicken tenders in the cereal crumbs and coat well; shake off the excess. Next, dip each piece in the egg-sauce mixture, coating well, then dip in the cereal mixture a second time, coating well.

Heat the oil in a large, heavy skillet over medium-high heat to 325°F.

Drop the coated chicken tenders carefully into the hot oil and cook until golden brown and fully cooked through, flipping over once, 3 to 5 minutes total per tender.

Drain and serve immediately with more sauce on the side if you like.

six

SWIMMERS

BARBECUE SHRIMP COCKTAIL

FINGER-LICKIN' BARBECUE SHRIMP-AND-CHEESE GRITS

BARBECUE BACON-WRAPPED SCALLOPS

PITMASTER-STYLE SMOKED SCALLOPS WITH SLAW

REAL-DILL LEMON TILAPIA

GRILLED CLAMS WITH BARBECUE BUTTER AND BAGUETTE

BARBECUE TUNA STEAKS

BLACKENED BARBECUE CATFISH

SMOKY CATFISH TACOS

SMOKED BLUEFISH SPREAD

BARBECUE SMOKED SALMON

GRILLED COD KEBABS

It surprises people to discover exactly how much I know about fish. We all know barbecue is so associated with meat—and where I'm from hog in particular. But it's possible to know nearly as much about the bass as about the pig. That's because I grew up fishing, being toted along by my father as he practiced his favorite pastime. I cannot tell you how many hours of my childhood were whiled away on the banks of the Flint River in rural southwest Georgia.

I learned to cook fish because we caught a lot—at least once a week, thanks to Jack "The Fishing King" Mixon. Catfish, bream, perch, mullet, Gulf sturgeon, shoal bass—you name it; if it swims in the Apalachicola River system, then I've eaten a ton of it. We usually prepared it in the style of a good old-fashioned Sunday fish fry, which is to say dredged in cornmeal and golden fried until it's crisp, moist, tender, and melting.

Around 1996, when I quit all of my jobs and began devoting my life to professional barbecue cooking, I will tell you I didn't see a place for fish cooking in it. I was on the road nearly all the time, pulling my rig from competition to competition, jiggering and rejiggering my recipes for my world-famous ribs (Ribs the Easy Way see page 35) and other specialties. But along the way I figured some things out: First of all, I saw that there were other ways to prepare fish than frying it. Fish is a natural for smoking because most of it is subtly flavored and thus picks up the essence of the smoke quite readily.

Of course, one of the many hazards of life on the road—and you can ask anyone who has ever played minor league ball or guitar in a rock band and he'll tell you the same—is that you're likely to gain weight. I also discovered that. But you can bet that I'm not giving up my love of outdoor cooking, of grilled and smoked foods. I came late to the party of folks who already knew that smoking and grilling fish are among the healthiest ways of preparing it—there's no grease, no butter, no oil, and so no added fat. But now I'm here, and I'm enjoying myself, because it's damn delicious.

I've discovered something that I hope you either already know or are open-minded enough to find out: Cooking fish on the grill or smoker is smart because it allows the flavorings and seasonings to shine. It gives you a chance to experiment with seasoning your food—in fact, you have to or it won't taste good. So have at it. Thank me later for the pounds you'll drop and the guests you'll surprise when you bring out that beautiful smoked salmon or the grilled shrimp cocktail. Or you can thank me now if you like.

Barbecue Shrimp Cocktail

You think I can't take any classic dish and put a barbecue spin on it? Here is proof that I can: I love a big ole shrimp cocktail, but I smoke mine and replace the cocktail sauce with barbecue sauce. It's a whole new dish, possibly better than the original. It makes an excellent appetizer, of course, but also goes well with a tossed green salad and some good crusty bread.

Note: If you are using wooden skewers, soak them in water for 30 minutes before using to prevent them from burning on the grill.

Serves 4 to 6

Shrimp

1½ pounds large shrimp, peeled and deveined

1 teaspoon garlic powder

2 teaspoons Only Rub (page 22)

2 tablespoons olive oil

2 tablespoons fresh lemon juice

Cocktail sauce

1 cup Only Sauce (page 24)

¼ cup prepared horseradish

1 tablespoon Worcestershire sauce

1 teaspoon Louisiana-style hot sauce

Salt and freshly ground pepper if needed

Place the shrimp, garlic powder, and rub in a medium bowl and toss to mix. Stir in the olive oil and lemon juice and marinate for 30 minutes.

Prepare the cocktail sauce: Place all the ingredients in a small bowl and whisk to mix.

Taste and add salt and pepper if needed. Divide the sauce among 4 to 6 tiny bowls or ramekins.

Heat a charcoal grill (see page 4) or gas grill (see page 5) to high heat.

Thread the shrimp (3 to 4) onto skewers. Grill the shrimp uncovered until cooked through, about 2 minutes per side. Remove from the grill and immediately place 2 or 3 skewers on each plate with a ramekin of cocktail sauce.

Finger-Lickin' Barbecue Shrimp-and-Cheese Grits

Shrimp and grits is a Southern staple, especially in the "lowland" places like Charleston and Savannah, where they have plenty of access to fresh seafood. It was likely born there as a classic "poor man's dish" made with whatever ingredients were plentiful at the time of year. And now shrimp and grits is an exalted thing; even fancy joints for yuppies in Brooklyn, New York, serve it! What's great about shrimp and grits is the combination of sweet seafood with the earthy softness of the cornmeal. My version is spiked with my hickory sauce, and my secret ingredient to keep everything light and fresh is, believe it or not, a dose of lager beer.

Serves 4

$3/4$ cup quick-cooking grits
Salt and freshly ground black pepper
2 tablespoons unsalted butter
2 ounces sharp white cheddar cheese, shredded (about ¾ cup)
2 tablespoons canola oil
¾ cup Only Other Sauce (page 25)
1 pound shelled and deveined medium shrimp
¼ cup lager beer, preferably Stella

Make the cheese grits: Bring 3 cups of water to a boil in a medium saucepan. Gradually add the grits and a generous pinch of salt. Reduce the heat to low, cover, and cook, stirring occasionally, until the grits are thick and porridge-like, about 7 minutes. Season with salt and pepper, stir in the butter, and finally stir in the cheese until it is melted. Cover the grits and keep warm.

Make the shrimp: In a large skillet, heat the canola oil with the sauce over medium heat until hot but not bubbling, about 30 seconds. Add the shrimp, season with salt and pepper, and cook until the shrimp are opaque, about 2 minutes. Add the beer and cook until the shrimp are white throughout and the sauce is slightly reduced, 2 to 4 minutes more. Spoon the grits into bowls, top with the shrimp and sauce, and serve.

Barbecue Bacon-Wrapped Scallops

Angels on horseback or oysters en brochette is an appetizer of shucked oysters wrapped in bacon, skewered, and broiled. This is my idea for how to make it, only I make it with scallops instead—which are a bit more durable on the grill, a bit meatier in texture, and really take on a smoky flavor.

Note: If using wooden skewers, soak them in water for 30 minutes before using to prevent them from burning on the grill.

Serves 4 as an appetizer

2 tablespoons vegetable oil
8 slices bacon
8 large sea scallops (about 1 pound)
½ cup Only Other Sauce (page 25)
1 teaspoon Only Other Rub (page 23)

Heat a charcoal grill (see page 4) or gas grill (see page 5) to medium-high heat.

In a large skillet, heat the vegetable oil over medium heat until shimmering. Add the bacon and cook, turning, until it just begins to crisp, 5 to 7 minutes. Alternately, cook the bacon in the microwave: Dampen 4 or 5 paper towels and line a microwave-safe plate with them. Place the bacon on the paper towel–covered plate. Microwave on high for about 2½ minutes, just until the bacon starts to cook but is not crisp. Let the bacon cool slightly.

Wrap 1 bacon slice around each scallop. Thread 2 scallops onto each of 4 wooden or metal skewers.

Place on the grill and grill uncovered for 7 to 8 minutes, until the scallops are cooked through and the bacon is crisp, turning frequently and brushing with the sauce. Transfer to a platter and sprinkle with the rub. Serve immediately.

Pitmaster-Style Smoked Scallops with Slaw

Smoked scallops are a great ingredient to have around; make some extra and you can store them in the fridge for up to two weeks. You can serve these beauties in any number of ways: tossed with linguine in a spicy garlic-tomato sauce; diced and added to a crock of creamy, potato-rich New England–style clam chowder; mixed with chopped bacon, mayonnaise, sour cream, and chives for a killer *Monday Night Football* dip . . . or try them this way, pitmaster-style, and that just means nice and smoky and on top of some cooling, tart coleslaw.

Serves 4 as an appetizer or 2 as a main course

8 large scallops (about 1 pound)

1 tablespoon plus 1 teaspoon Only Rub
   (page 22)

¼ cup fresh lemon juice

3 tablespoons olive oil

2 tablespoons sour cream or Greek yogurt

3 cups finely grated iceberg lettuce
   (about 1 large head)

Season the scallops on both sides with about half of the rub, reserving the rest.

Prepare a smoker with soaked wood chips and heat it to 300°F (see page 6). Alternatively, prepare a charcoal grill (see page 7) or gas grill (see page 8) for smoking and heat it to medium heat.

Place the scallops on the side of the rack (not directly over where the chips will be smoking), leaving enough room around them so all sides smoke evenly. Place the lid on the smoker, leaving about 2 inches uncovered.

As soon as the smoker gets to 300°F cover the smoker with the lid and let the heat drop to medium-low, about 250°F, which will take about 5 minutes. Smoke the scallops just until they firm up slightly and are barely opaque in the center, about 15 minutes.

Meanwhile, make the slaw: In a medium bowl, whisk together the lemon juice, olive oil, sour cream, and remaining rub. Place the grated lettuce in a large bowl and pour the dressing over it; toss to coat.

Divide the slaw among 4 plates, top each with 2 smoked scallops, and serve immediately.

Real-Dill Lemon Tilapia

I've heard tilapia referred to as "America's favorite fish," and I can tell you that it's certainly one of my own. It has a nice subtle flavor, a firm texture that can stand up to the grill or smoker, and because it's so widely farmed it's not too expensive. I like to combine it with lots of fresh lemon juice and dill, and then I add some hickory-tinged rub.

Serves 4

Juice of 1 large lemon

2 tablespoons olive oil

1 tablespoon chopped fresh dill, or 1 teaspoon dried dill

1 teaspoon Only Rub (page 22)

½ teaspoon Dijon mustard

Four 6-ounce tilapia fillets

In a medium bowl, whisk together all of the ingredients except the fish. Pour into a large zip-top bag, add the fish, seal the bag, and turn the fish to coat. Place in the refrigerator to marinate for 30 to 45 minutes.

Heat a charcoal grill (see page 4) or gas grill (see page 5) to medium-high heat.

Place the fish in a shallow aluminum pan. Place the pan on the grill and cook, covered, for 12 to 14 minutes, until the fish is just cooked through and flakes easily with a fork. Remove from the grill and serve immediately.

Grilled Clams with Barbecue Butter and Baguette

Juicy, briny, grilled clams, just made to be sopped with some good crusty bread. These clams can be put together easily in less than a half hour.

Serves 4 as an appetizer or 2 as a main course

4 tablespoons (½ stick) unsalted butter, softened
1 tablespoon Only Other Rub (page 23)
1 tablespoon fresh lemon juice
1 good baguette or other French bread, cut into about 8 thick slices
2 pounds Manila clams, well scrubbed

Heat a charcoal grill (see page 4) or gas grill (see page 5) to high heat.

In a small bowl, combine the softened butter with the rub and lemon juice. Using a butter knife, thinly spread the butter on 1 side of each bread slice (plenty of butter will remain).

Arrange the clams in a single layer in a cast iron pan or a disposable aluminum pan. Place the pan on the grill, cover, and cook just until clams open, 8 to 10 minutes (discard any clams that do not open). Using a slotted spoon, transfer the grilled clams to 2 or 4 shallow bowls. Grill the bread until slightly charred, 1 to 2 minutes per side. Put the remaining butter in the aluminum pan and place it on the grill; stir until melted. Pour the juices from the pan over the clams. Serve with the grilled buttered bread.

Barbecue Tuna Steaks

Lots of folks try to tell you that tuna tastes like steak. If what you really want is a steak, turn to page 83. Tuna doesn't taste like steak, but on the grill a big old hunk of it sure does act like red meat—and it's for that reason that I like to use my rub and minimal other seasonings to make it wake up and scream. Cooked like this, tuna can be (nearly) as great as any steak. You can even serve it up with mashed potatoes if you want to.

Serves 2

1 tablespoon fresh lemon juice
1½ teaspoons olive oil
1 tablespoon Only Other Sauce (page 25)
Two 6-ounce tuna steaks
¼ teaspoon kosher salt
¼ teaspoon freshly ground black pepper
1 teaspoon Only Rub (page 22)

In a large zip-top bag, combine the lemon juice, olive oil, and sauce. Add the tuna, seal the bag, and turn the fish to coat. Refrigerate for up to 30 minutes, turning occasionally.

Remove the tuna from the bag and sprinkle with the salt, pepper, and rub.

Heat a charcoal grill (see page 4) or gas grill (see page 5) to medium-high heat.

Grill the tuna, covered, for 3 to 4 minutes on each side for medium-rare (until slightly pink in the center). Remove from the grill and let rest for 5 minutes before serving.

Blackened Barbecue Catfish

To blacken a fish just means to coat it in spices and cook it at such a high heat that the spices form a deep dark crust on the outside, searing in the juices and moisture. This fish is very easy to prepare, and it's a great way of bringing traditional barbecue flavors to an indoor cooking technique. You can use this recipe for any similar fish such as flounder or bass as well.

Serves 4

Four 6-ounce catfish fillets
2 tablespoons Only Rub (page 22)
2 tablespoons peanut oil
Rice for serving
Only Slaw (page 37) for serving, optional

Heat a charcoal grill (see page 4) to medium-high heat and preheat a cast-iron skillet over the hot coals.

Cover both sides of the fish with the rub. Pour the peanut oil into the skillet and heat it until hot, about 3 minutes. Lay the fish in the skillet and close the grill.

Cook the fish for about 4 minutes, then turn and cook, uncovered, for about another 4 minutes, until both sides are well seared and crusted with the spices. Remove from pan and serve immediately, over rice and with slaw, if you like.

Make it on the stovetop: Preheat a cast-iron skillet over medium heat and pour in the peanut oil. When the oil is hot, add the fish and cover the pan, then follow the cooking directions above.

Smoky Catfish Tacos

A good Baja-style fish taco involves fried fish with a creamy sauce and shredded cabbage all wrapped in a tortilla. But who says you can't have barbecue tacos? A good pitmaster-style fish taco contains smoked fish with a creamy slaw wrapped in a tortilla—same deal, if you see what I mean. And it's just as fun to eat because you get to roll your own and pick it up with your hands.

Serves 4

1½ pounds catfish fillets (about 4 fillets)
1 tablespoon Only Rub (page 22)
2 large ripe tomatoes, finely diced
¼ large onion, finely diced
¼ cup finely chopped cilantro
1 jalapeño pepper, seeded and finely diced
1 tablespoon cider vinegar
1 garlic clove, minced
Coarse salt
¾ cup Only Sauce (page 24)
8 corn tortillas
1 tablespoon vegetable oil
8 ounces prepackaged shredded coleslaw mix (4 cups)
1 tablespoon fresh lime juice
2 tablespoons sour cream
Freshly ground black pepper

Coat the catfish fillets with the rub. Lay the fillets in a large aluminum foil pan, cover, and marinate in the refrigerator for at least 3 hours or overnight.

Make the salsa: In a large bowl combine the tomatoes, onions, cilantro, jalapeños, vinegar, garlic, and ¾ teaspoon salt. Cover and refrigerate until ready to serve.

continued

Prepare a smoker with soaked wood chips and heat it to 180°F (see page 6). Alternatively, prepare a charcoal grill (see page 7) or gas grill (see page 8) for smoking and heat it to low heat.

Cook the catfish in the aluminum pan on the top rack of the smoker for about 1 hour, covered, opening the smoker only to brush the fish with the sauce every 20 minutes. The catfish is done when it is flaky and white on the inside. Remove the fish from the smoker and let rest, covered, while setting up the tacos.

Lightly brush the tortillas with the vegetable oil. Stack the tortillas, wrap them in foil, and put them in the smoker to warm through, 2 to 3 minutes.

Meanwhile, make the slaw: In a medium bowl, combine the shredded coleslaw mix with the lime juice and sour cream and season with salt and pepper. Toss well.

Flake the catfish and place it on a platter with the warmed tortillas and serve with the salsa and slaw.

Smoked Bluefish Spread

Bluefish makes a lot of people think of summer in New England, but these suckers roam the whole Atlantic far beyond Nantucket: They swim all the way down to Georgia, where I live, and they're fairly easy to get your hands on. When you find them, they're oily, richly flavored, and often inexpensive—but spoil quickly. A lot of the Long Island crowd make a fancy spread they call "bluefish pâté," which is excellent on toast or crackers. My version relies on smoking the fish, which makes it last longer, and turning it into a smoky-spiced spread that's perfect for munching at a backyard barbecue or family lunch while you wait for the burgers to come off the grill.

Serves 6 to 8 as an appetizer

1 teaspoon salt	1 tablespoon Worcestershire sauce
1 teaspoon freshly ground black pepper	1 tablespoon fresh lemon juice
1 teaspoon Only Other Rub (page 23)	1 tablespoon chopped parsley
1 pound skinless, boneless bluefish fillets	½ medium red onion, minced
3 tablespoons olive oil	4 dashes of hot sauce, or to taste
8 ounces cream cheese, softened	Crackers or toasts for serving

Smoke the fish: Combine the salt, pepper, and rub in a small bowl. Coat the bluefish fillets with 1 tablespoon of the olive oil and the spice mixture.

Prepare a smoker with soaked wood chips and heat it to 325°F (see page 6). Alternatively, prepare a charcoal grill (see page 7) or gas grill (see page 8) for smoking and heat it to medium heat.

Lay the bluefish on the smoker's rack. Cover and smoke for 12 to 14 minutes, until the fish is flaky and white on the inside. Remove the fish from the smoker and loosely cover until you are ready to make the spread.

Make the spread: In a bowl, blend the remaining olive oil with the cream cheese, Worcestershire sauce, lemon juice, parsley, onions, and hot sauce. Flake the smoked bluefish into the cream cheese mixture and fold it in. Serve in a crock or bowl alongside crackers or toast.

Barbecue Smoked Salmon

You want some happy guests at your next barbecue? Instead of serving up ribs or chicken, give them a huge fillet of salmon—they'll feel virtuous as they chow down, and they'll also enjoy the unexpected kick that the rub and sauce lend this velvety smooth and sweetly flavored fish. I like to smoke the fish with applewood to pair nicely with the cure and rub. The curing process not only adds flavor to the fish but also helps preserve it, though it does take some advance planning. Start on Saturday and have everybody over for Sunday.

Serves 10 to 12

½ cup granulated sugar
½ cup light brown sugar
⅓ cup kosher salt
2 tablespoons freshly ground black pepper
Two 2-pound center-cut salmon fillets, skin on and pin bones removed, about
    1½ inches thick each
1½ to 3 tablespoons Only Other Rub (page 23)
1 cup Only Other Sauce (page 25) for serving

Get out a baking sheet large enough to hold your salmon fillets. Lay a thin sheet of foil on the baking sheet, and then lay a thin sheet of plastic wrap on top of the foil.

Make the cure: In a medium bowl, thoroughly combine the sugars, salt, and pepper. Sprinkle a third of the cure onto the plastic wrap, roughly the length of one fillet. Lay the fillet skin side down onto the cure and then sprinkle another third of the cure onto the flesh. Stack the second fillet skin side down onto the coated flesh of the first fillet. Sprinkle the last third of the cure on top of this fillet, then cover with another sheet of plastic wrap and more foil.

Wrap the plastic wrap and foil tightly around the fish. This will contain any oils or juices that may escape during the curing process. Set another baking sheet on top of the foil-wrapped fish and weigh it down with something heavy like a few cookbooks or canned goods.

Refrigerate the salmon for 8 to 10 hours to cure. If your fillet is particularly thin (less than an inch), go for about 8 hours; if it's thicker, you can go up to about 10 hours. Try not to cure for more than 12 hours, especially if your taste buds are sensitive to salt. It helps to set a timer to go off after 8 hours.

Remove the fish from the fridge and unwrap the foil. You should be greeted by a bright red, juicy piece of fish. Thoroughly rinse off the fish under cold water, making sure to wash off any of the cure that hasn't been absorbed into the fish.

Pat both fillets dry with napkins or paper towels. Pat 1½ tablespoons of the rub onto one of the fillets to form a thin layer. Dust off any excess. Repeat with the second fillet, or leave the second fillet unseasoned to give dinner guests an option.

Allow the fillets to dry at room temperature for 1 to 3 hours to form the pellicle: This is a thin, dry, matte-like film on the surface of the fish that helps the smoke better adhere to the meat. It's hard to tell when this is done when the fish is covered with the dry rub; you can use an unseasoned fish to judge when this process is complete or leave a small portion of one of the fillets free of dry rub.

As the fish finishes drying, prepare a smoker with soaked wood chips and heat it to 150°F (see page 6). Alternatively, prepare a charcoal grill (see page 7) or gas grill (see page 8) for smoking and heat it to low heat.

You want your smoker to maintain a consistent temperature of 150°F for the whole time. This low temperature can be difficult to achieve with some smokers, so make sure you dial back the fuel a bit by adding less charcoal and hardwood than you typically would for higher-temperature smoking.

Lay the salmon fillets side by side and skin side down in the smoker. Depending on how many pounds of fish you're cooking and the thickness of the fish, the smoking

continued

process can take anywhere from 1 to 3 hours. Cooking is complete when the salmon registers 140°F at its thickest point.

Once the fish reaches 140°F, take it off the smoker and put it on a baking sheet. Tent with foil and allow the fish to rest for 20 to 30 minutes, which will raise its temperature another 5 degrees and let the muscles relax and the juices redistribute.

Remove the tented foil and serve immediately, with the sauce on the side.

Grilled Cod Kebabs

I love cod because it's a firm-fleshed white fish that's easy to deal with and has plenty of meaty bite when you eat it—in other words, great for kebabs. These are fragrant with herbs, guaranteed to make your mouth water. And because you marinate them in advance, when it comes time for cooking all you have to do is throw them on the grill.

Serves 4

2 medium onions, finely chopped
2 large garlic cloves, finely chopped
1 jalapeño pepper, finely chopped
2 tablespoons dried dill, or ½ cup fresh chopped dill
2 tablespoons dried parsley, or ½ cup chopped fresh parsley
1 tablespoon Only Rub (page 22)
1 cup beer, preferably a pale lager such as Stella Artois
4 pounds black cod, cut into 2-inch pieces
Vegetable oil for brushing
Salt and freshly ground black pepper
Lemon wedges for serving

In a large bowl, toss the onions with the garlic, jalapeños, dill, parsley, rub, and beer. Add the fish and toss to coat thoroughly with the marinade. Cover and refrigerate for about 4 hours.

Heat a charcoal grill (see page 4) or gas grill (see page 5) to high heat.

Thread the fish onto 8 metal skewers, leaving a small space between each piece. Brush the fish with vegetable oil and season with salt and pepper. Grill, turning occasionally, until lightly charred and just opaque throughout, about 12 minutes total. Serve 2 kebabs per person, with lemon wedges on the side.

seven

DRUNKEN RECIPES

SMOKED RIB EYES WITH BOURBON BUTTER

THE BOURBON-BACON BURGER

SMOKED WHISKEY WINGS

BOURBON BROWN SUGAR CHICKEN

SMOKED TURKEY WITH WHISKEY GRAVY

WHISKEY GRILLED SHRIMP

BOURBON SMOKED SALMON

BOURBON'D SWEET POTATO CASSEROLE

WHISKEY CREAMED CORN

know what you're thinking: These are the recipes I came up with late one night when I could barely stand up and inspiration struck me as hard as the whiskey I'd been working on for a few hours. But you'd be wrong. These are the recipes that combine two of my favorite things—barbecue and whiskey—and together they make for some great dishes.

You want to make your food *really* taste good? Think about building a "flavor profile." I know that term drives some folks crazy. It's overused and misused. But that doesn't mean the advice isn't sound.

Here's what flavor profile means to me, Myron Mixon: It's a simple concept that refers to the *layers* of flavor of whatever you're eating. The first thing you do is start at the foundation, the base flavor of whatever you're cooking. Let's say it's meat. You'll want to start by focusing on the natural flavor of the meat and highlight that. On top of the meat flavor you may next want the marinade and the rub and the sauce to announce their presence. Finally, and just as important, is the flavor of the smoke. Together these are the layers of taste or flavor profile of the dish.

The way whiskey fits into this is that just a touch is a great way to add depth to a dish and ultimately make it more delicious.

What do I mean when I say whiskey? The term "whiskey" is actually a generic one. It means, simply, distilled liquor made from fermented mashed-up grains. Whiskey can mean bourbon, Tennessee whiskey, Scotch whiskey, Irish whiskey, and my favorite of all whiskies, Canadian. Each of these whiskies has it own character, its own governing guidelines for how it's made, and its own distillation process.

In the most general terms (I know there are always exceptions to these rules), Scotch is known for the smoky flavor it derives from peat moss. Irish whiskey has a more barley-malt flavor and typically very little smoke. And by law, for a whiskey to be labeled "straight bourbon whiskey," the mashed grain must contain at least 51 percent corn, be distilled at no more than 160 proof, and be aged in new, charred oak barrels for a minimum of two years. That's what gives bourbon its distinctive smoky-sweetness, and why people like to cook with it (to impart that signature flavor into their food). Now Jack Daniel's is something different: This is a "sour-mash Tennessee whiskey," which means that a portion of the previous day's mash has been added to this day's blend of fermented mashed-up grains, and that the mash has then been filtered through sugar/maple charcoal. (The process is different enough that Tennessee whiskey cannot be called bourbon, although for most people the two are similar in taste and thus can be used interchangeably in recipes.) Finally, Canadian whiskey is prized by enthusiasts (like me) for its smoothness, its amber color, and its mellow, straightforward, light, and clear fruit flavor.

Trendy ingredients come and go, and I'm usually not one to follow them too closely. A lot of times what's trendy doesn't even make sense when it comes to barbecue. (I see a lot of recipes for kale lately. I don't care how wonderful kale is for you; I'm just not going to put it on my smoker. I might, however, use it to garnish and decorate a whole hog for competition because I like its curly edges.) Whiskies aren't ever going to be out of fashion, and they can be counted on to add some interesting flavor to your food. Come see how it's done. And of course I encourage you to sample a little on the side.

Smoked Rib Eyes with Bourbon Butter

If there's a pleasure in life better than a perfectly grilled steak with a strong cocktail, I'm not sure I know about it. (OK, well, maybe making money winning a competition at the same time you're enjoying those two things, I'll give you that.) Here's an excellent way to combine your enjoyments.

Note: The bourbon butter can be made and refrigerated for up to a week in advance.

Serves 4

½ cup (1 stick) unsalted butter, softened
1 to 2 cloves garlic, finely minced
2 tablespoons bourbon
1 tablespoon finely minced scallion
1 teaspoon dried parsley
1 tablespoon plus 1 teaspoon Only Rub (page 22)
4 rib eye steaks, each at least 1 inch thick

In a small bowl, combine the butter, garlic, bourbon, scallions, parsley, and 1 teaspoon of the rub. Mash together with a fork until well combined. Set aside.

Prepare a smoker with soaked wood chips and heat it to 500°F (see page 6). Alternatively, prepare a charcoal grill (see page 7) or gas grill (see page 8) for smoking and heat it to high heat.

Season the steaks liberally on both sides with the remaining 1 tablespoon rub.

Place the steaks on the grill rack, cover, and smoke them for 3 to 4 minutes per side for medium rare. (Add about 2 minutes for medium.) Transfer the steaks to a platter and cover with aluminum foil. Let rest for 5 minutes.

Place each steak on a plate, top with a pat of the bourbon butter, and serve.

The Bourbon-Bacon Burger

I'm always interested in making burgers that are a little juicier, a little more flavorful, and a little more naturally salty so that the meat's flavor comes out. By combining a bit of bourbon and smoky chopped bacon into the meat mixture, I've done it. These burgers will knock your friends' socks off at your next backyard barbecue.

Makes 4 burgers

1½ lbs. 80% lean ground chuck
4 slices bacon, cooked and crumbled
2 tablespoons bourbon
1 tablespoon Worcestershire sauce
1 tablespoon Only Rub (page 22)
4 slices pepper Jack cheese
4 soft hamburger buns, split
1 to 2 tablespoons softened butter for the buns
Only Sauce (page 24) for serving, optional
4 large romaine lettuce leaves for serving, optional
4 thick ripe tomato slices for serving, optional

Heat a charcoal grill (see page 4) or gas grill (see page 5) to medium-high heat.

In a large bowl, combine the meat with the bacon, bourbon, Worcestershire sauce, and rub and mix gently with your hands to combine, taking care not to overmix. Separate the meat mixture into 4 even portions and form them into patties.

Grill the burgers, covered, until cooked through, 5 to 7 minutes depending on desire doneness, flipping them about halfway through the cooking time. (Do *not* press down on them with your spatula.) After you flip the burgers, add the cheese so it can melt.

Place bun halves cut side down on the grill and toast until lightly golden, 1 to 2 minutes. Remove the buns from the grill and butter them. Place a cheeseburger in each bun. Serve immediately, with sauce, lettuce, and tomato slices on the burgers if you like.

Smoked Whiskey Wings

You got your breast men and your leg men and your thigh men, but let me tell you something: I'm a wing man. What I love about wings is that you get a two-in-one treat when you eat them: Between the drumette and the flat, that's some good gnawing. Wings are great for weeknight cooking too, because they take very little time to prepare and cook.

NOTE: The best way to trim chicken wings is to use kitchen shears to lop off the tips and separate the pieces.

Serves 4 to 6 as an appetizer

2 dozen whole chicken wings
Kosher salt and freshly ground pepper
¾ cup Only Sauce (page 24), plus more for serving, optional
¼ cup whiskey
1 tablespoon sugar
¼ cup plus 2 tablespoons Dijon mustard

Using kitchen shears or a very sharp knife, cut each wing in half to separate the flat from the drumette; cut off and discard the tip or save it for stock. Wash the pieces well, pat them dry, season liberally with salt and pepper, and set them aside in a large zip-top freezer bag.

In a small saucepan, whisk the sauce with the whiskey and sugar and bring just to a simmer over medium-high heat. Remove the sauce from the heat and whisk in the mustard. Cool completely. Pour the mixture in the bag with the chicken wings, seal the bag, and marinate in the refrigerator for at least 30 minutes or up to overnight.

Prepare a smoker with soaked wood chips and heat it to 250°F (see page 6). Alternatively, prepare a charcoal grill (see page 7) or gas grill (see page 8) for smoking and heat it to medium-low heat.

Remove the wings from the marinade and discard the marinade. Place the wings in a large, shallow aluminum pan in a single layer. Place the uncovered pan in the smoker and cook, for 2 hours. Remove the wings from the smoker and serve with more sauce on the side if you like.

Bourbon Brown Sugar Chicken

You need the sweetness of the bourbon here to help complement the naturally clean flavor of the boneless skinless chicken breasts. Worcestershire sauce and brown sugar intensify this experience. Many of us are choosing boneless skinless chicken breasts for dinner because they're high in protein and low in calories, but this choice can be a bit boring. Combining appealing flavors and the smoke from the grill ups the deliciousness of the chicken breast in this recipe.

Serves 4

¼ cup Only Sauce (page 24)
¼ cup bourbon
¼ cup dark brown sugar
1 teaspoon Worcestershire sauce
1 teaspoon salt
4 to 6 boneless, skinless chicken breast halves (about 2 pounds), pounded evenly to about ¼ inch thick
Pitmaster-Style Grilled Veggie Kebabs (page 247) for serving, optional

In a zip-top freezer bag, combine the sauce, bourbon, brown sugar, Worcestershire sauce, and salt. Place the chicken in the bag, turning to coat. Seal the bag and marinate in the refrigerator for at least 30 minutes or up to 2 hours.

Heat a charcoal grill (see page 4) or gas grill (see page 5) to medium heat.

Remove the chicken from the marinade and discard the marinade. Grill the chicken uncovered for 6 to 7 minutes per side, until cooked through. Serve with Pitmaster-Style Veggie Kebabs if you like.

Make it in the oven: Marinate the chicken as directed above. Preheat the oven to 400°F, remove the chicken breasts from the marinade, and discard the marinade. Place the chicken on a nonstick baking sheet and bake, turning once, until cooked through and golden brown, about 30 minutes.

Smoked Turkey with Whiskey Gravy

One word: Thanksgiving. Your grandkids will be telling *their* grandkids about this delicious turkey.

Serves 8 to 10

One 12- to 15-pound turkey, neck and giblets removed
11½ cups chicken stock
3 medium white onions, diced
4 gloves garlic, crushed
1 cup packed dark brown sugar
2 cups Only Rub (page 22)
¾ cup all-purpose flour
½ cup whiskey
Salt and freshly ground black pepper

Rinse the turkey inside and out and pat it dry thoroughly. Place the turkey in a large roasting bag and add 8 cups of the stock, the onions, garlic, and brown sugar. Seal the bag and place it in a large roasting pan. Place in the refrigerator to marinate overnight.

When you are ready to cook the turkey, prepare a smoker with soaked wood chips and heat it to 250°F (see page 6). Alternatively, prepare a charcoal grill (see page 7) or gas grill (see page 8) for smoking and heat it to medium-low heat.

Remove the turkey from the bag and discard the marinade. Apply the rub all over the bird. Put the turkey on a rack in a large, deep aluminum pan, place the pan in the smoker, cover, and cook for 5 hours, or until the breast meat reaches an internal temperature of 165°F.

Remove the pan from the smoker. Allow the turkey to rest, loosely covered with foil, for 30 minutes.

Meanwhile, make the gravy: Pour the remaining pan juices from the aluminum pan into a bowl and skim the fat, reserving 6 tablespoons of the fat for the gravy. Reserve all the defatted pan juices.

In a large saucepan, mix the fat with the flour to form a paste.

In a medium saucepan, whisk the remaining 3½ cups stock with the whiskey and slowly whisk the mixture into the flour paste. Bring to a boil over medium heat, whisking constantly. Whisk in the reserved pan juices, reduce the heat to low, and simmer, whisking frequently, until thickened and flavorful, about 25 minutes. Season with salt and pepper. Transfer to a large gravy boat. Carve the turkey, arrange on a platter, and serve with the whiskey gravy.

Whiskey Grilled Shrimp

I love making shrimp skewers because my guests find them festive and special, and because I find them very easy. Killer combination: easy to cook, easy to eat. Shrimp's sweet flavor is wonderful with the deeper, more intense sweetness of whiskey. Or you could use any type of whiskey you like; Jack Daniel's, with its fiery bite, is another good choice.

NOTE: If using wooden skewers, soak them in water for 30 minutes before using to prevent them from burning on the grill.

Serves 4 to 6

2 tablespoons unsalted butter
1½ cups Only Sauce (page 24)
¼ cup whiskey
3 tablespoons cider vinegar
2 tablespoons molasses
2 tablespoons honey
2 dashes of Louisiana-style hot sauce
2 pounds peeled and deveined large shrimp

Melt the butter in a medium saucepan over low heat. Stir in the sauce, whiskey, vinegar, molasses, honey, and hot sauce. Bring to a simmer and simmer until thickened, about 40 minutes. Remove from the heat and let the sauce cool to room temperature.

Pour the cooled sauce into a large zip-top freezer bag and toss the shrimp to coat. Seal and marinate for about 15 minutes at room temperature.

Heat a charcoal grill (see page 4) or gas grill (see page 5) to high heat.

Thread the shrimp onto metal or wooden skewers, 3 shrimp per skewer. Discard the marinade.

Grill the shrimp uncovered until cooked through, about 2 minutes per side. Remove from the heat and serve the shrimp over grits, a green salad, linguine tossed with garlic and butter, or any dish you like.

Bourbon Smoked Salmon

Folks these days are all trying to eat more fish, myself included. When I was growing up there was only way to eat fish: fried in cornmeal. That sure is good, but it's definitely not the most healthful. This hot-smoked salmon is healthier and tastier all around. Salmon sometimes can have a fishy flavor because of its high oil content. A brief soak in bourbon helps remove this fishy flavor, and in its place infuses some natural sweetness to complement the fish's essence.

Serves 4 to 6

1 to 1½ pounds skinless center-cut salmon fillet
1 cup bourbon
1 cup dark brown sugar
½ cup kosher or coarse sea salt
2 tablespoons freshly ground black pepper
1 tablespoon ground coriander
Bagels and cream cheese or toast points, capers, and sour cream for serving

Wash the salmon fillet under cold running water and blot it dry with paper towels. Run your fingers over the fillet, feeling for bones; pull out any you find with needle-nose pliers. Place the fish in a baking dish, pour the bourbon over it, and turn to coat. Marinate the salmon in the refrigerator for 20 minutes, turning it twice.

Place the brown sugar, salt, pepper, and coriander in a medium bowl and mix well, breaking up any lumps in the sugar.

Drain the fish and blot it dry with paper towels. Wipe out the baking dish. Spread one third of the brown sugar mixture in the bottom of the baking dish in the shape of the fish fillet. Place the fish in the dish, and top with the remaining brown sugar mixture. Cover with plastic wrap and cure the fish in the refrigerator for 4 hours. When properly cured, you'll notice a pool of liquid at the bottom of the baking dish; this is the liquid the salt has drawn out of the fish.

Rinse the salmon under cold running water to wash off the cure. Blot it dry with paper towels.

Prepare a smoker with soaked wood chips and heat it to 250°F (see page 6). Alternatively, prepare a charcoal grill (see page 7) or gas grill (see page 8) for smoking and heat it to medium-low heat.

Arrange the salmon fillet, skin side down, on the smoker's rack. Cover the smoker and smoke until cooked through, about 18 minutes from start to finish. Use the flake test to check for doneness: Press the fish with your finger; when it's done it will break into clean flakes.

Transfer the fish to a wire rack set over a plate to cool to room temperature, then cover and refrigerate until ready to serve. (It tastes best served chilled.) Serve with bagels and cream cheese, or with toast points, capers, and sour cream.

Bourbon'd Sweet Potato Casserole

Sweet potatoes and bourbon go together like cake and ice cream, like peanut butter and jelly, like they were made for each other. They're both naturally earthy and, well, nice and sweet. If you want to put marshmallows on top of this and broil the casserole before serving it, you most certainly can.

Serves 6 to 8

8 medium sweet potatoes
2 pinches of salt
7 tablespoons unsalted butter
½ cup half-and-half
¼ cup bourbon
3 tablespoons dark brown sugar
1 cup mini marshmallows, optional

Preheat the oven to 350°F and butter a medium baking dish.

Put the sweet potatoes into a large pot, cover with cold water, and add the salt. Bring to a boil over high heat, then reduce the heat to medium and cook until soft when pierced, 30 to 40 minutes. Drain the sweet potatoes and set them aside to cool.

When cool enough to handle, peel the sweet potatoes and transfer the flesh to a large bowl. Coarsely mash the sweet potatoes with the tines of a fork, then add 5 tablespoons of the butter, the half-and-half, bourbon, and brown sugar. Beat with an electric mixer on medium speed until light and fluffy, about 2 minutes.

Transfer the sweet potato mixture to the prepared baking dish, dot with the remaining 2 tablespoons butter, and bake until the top is golden brown, about 30 minutes. If topping with mini marshmallows, spread them over the top, turn on the broiler, and broil for an additional 3 to 4 minutes, until browned on top. Serve immediately, while piping hot.

Whiskey Creamed Corn

This is a staple Southern side dish with some sin thrown in for good measure. The traditional version is often one note, meaning all you taste is the rich cream. If you want to make your creamed corn sing, spike it with a little whiskey, a handful of grated Parm, and the bite of garlic. Delicious.

Serves 6 to 8 as a side

4 tablespoons (½ stick) unsalted butter
1 cup chopped red onion (about 1 medium onion)
3 garlic cloves, minced
3 cups fresh or frozen corn kernels (from about 5 ears)
½ cup heavy cream
¼ cup whiskey
¼ cup grated Parmesan cheese
Salt and freshly ground black pepper
1 cup chopped red pepper for garnish, optional

Melt the butter in large, heavy skillet over medium heat. Add the onions and garlic and sauté for about 3 minutes, or until softened. Add the corn and sauté until almost tender, about 2 minutes more. Add ¼ cup of the cream and the whiskey. Bring to a simmer and simmer until the sauce thickens and coats the corn, stirring occasionally, about 4 minutes. Add the remaining ¼ cup cream and the Parmesan cheese. Return to a simmer and cook until the mixture thickens even more, 2 to 4 minutes. Season with salt and pepper. Transfer to a serving bowl and sprinkle with the red pepper, if using.

eight

BARBECUE BRUNCH

SLOW-SMOKED SUNDAY HAM

PITMASTER'S SMOKED EGGS BENEDICT WITH PULLED PORK CAKES

GRILLED EGG "MUFFINS"

BACKYARD BACON

GRILLED EGG-STUFFED PEPPERS

SMOKY BACON BLOODY MARY

SMOKY BACON DRY AND DIRTY VODKA MARTINIS

GRILLED HONEY-VANILLA FRENCH TOAST

BLUEBERRY-BUTTERMILK SWIRL GRILLED COFFEE CAKE

SMOKED EGG SALAD ENGLISH MUFFINS

f there's a meal that might not seem to fit with barbecue, it's probably brunch. After all, most people just want it to include good strong coffee, eggs cooked the way they like, smoky bacon, and a little something sweet on the side. I'm no different. But I make mine out back on my smoker. Seem crazy? Then you haven't been paying attention. This is what *Everyday Barbecue* is all about: incorporating your grill into your everyday life, not treating it like special-occasion cooking. There are few things that can't be done on the grill—even great eggs!

Right here and right now, let's change the notion that brunch is not typically associated with barbecuing and grilling. From the booze for the cocktails to French toast, and bacon, I'm going to show you recipes that will change the way you look at a late Sunday morning meal. If you're like me, you don't want to be trapped in a stuffy kitchen while your guests mill around waiting for you to finish cooking. You want to be out there with them, with a drink in your hand, presiding over the fire and smoke and the delicious foods cooking.

You'll find a few brunch staple recipes in this chapter, but most have been enhanced a bit—like my Smoky Bacon Bloody Mary (page 189) and Slow-Smoked Sunday Ham (page 179)—and you'll find some new favorites, like Grilled Egg "Muffins" (page 184), which are as good as any biscuit breakfast sandwich you'll have, and Pitmaster's Smoked Eggs Benedict with Pulled Pork Cake (page 181), which is served with an easy-to-make rejiggered barbecue-spiked hollandaise sauce. Some of these dishes, such as Backyard Bacon (page 186), might take a bit longer than other recipes in this book to prepare—but they are intended for slow weekend mornings when time is not always of the essence. After you host your first barbecue brunch, I'm sure you'll agree.

Slow-Smoked Sunday Ham

This is what I want to eat with eggs and biscuits at a late Sunday brunch. My version of honey-baked ham is a wonderful thing to behold. Note that by ham here I mean one that's already smoked and cured that you buy in the grocery store and not a raw never-been-touched ham that you get from a butcher shop. (If you smoke one of those, you get something that turns out like smoked pork shoulder, a barbecue dish; this is a different thing altogether.) A lot of people buy cured and smoked hams and then bake them in the oven at a low temperature for hours; a baked ham is a delicious thing, and I'll tell you how you can do it that way, but I highly recommend smoking this if you can—that extra bit of flavor puts this mild sweet meat right over the top.

Serves up to 30 people

One 15-pound precooked smoked ham on the bone
1½ cups apricot jam
1 cup Dijon mustard
1 cup firmly packed light brown sugar
½ cup Only Rub (page 22)

Prepare a smoker with soaked wood chips and heat it to 225°F (see page 6). Alternatively, prepare a charcoal grill (see page 7) or gas grill (see page 8) for smoking and heat it to medium-low heat.

Trim the tough outer skin and excess fat from the ham. Place the ham meat side down in a large aluminum foil pan, cover, and smoke the ham for 2 hours. Take it off the smoker.

Make a glaze by combining the jam, mustard, brown sugar, and rub in a medium bowl. Brush the ham with half of the glaze, put the ham back in the aluminum foil pan, cover it with foil, and return it to the smoker. Smoke the ham for about 1 hour more, or until the internal temperature is right around 145°F.

continued

Unwrap the foil covering the ham and baste it thoroughly with the remaining glaze.

Place the ham back in the smoker, cover, and smoke the ham for about 1 hour more. At this point the ham will be at least 145°F or maybe a little higher. Remove the ham from the smoker, loosely tent it with the foil, and allow it to rest for 30 minutes. Carve and serve warm or at room temperature.

Make it in the oven: Preheat the oven to 300°F. Trim the skin and fat from the ham as directed above. Place the ham meat side down in a large aluminum foil pan, cover, and roast it for 2 hours. Take the ham out of the oven and raise the oven temperature to 350°F. Make the glaze as directed above. Brush the ham with half of the glaze, put the ham back in the aluminum foil pan, cover it with foil, and return it to the oven. Cook for another 1½ hours, brushing with the remaining glaze halfway through the cooking time. Transfer to a cutting board or platter and rest, covered with the foil, for 30 minutes. Carve and serve warm or at room temperature.

Pitmaster's Smoked Eggs Benedict with Pulled Pork Cakes

I'm not going to lie: Traditional eggs Benedict is not easy to pull off. There are a lot of moving parts, and getting each component ready, on time and heated up properly, takes effort and practice. My barbecue version of this dish is a little bit easier all around. I use leftover pulled pork to make "cakes," I poach my eggs, and I whip together what I call cheater's hollandaise, a down-and-dirty take on the usual preparation.

Serves 4 to 8

Pork cakes

1 pound leftover barbecue pulled pork

1½ cups finely crushed Ritz crackers

2 large eggs

¼ cup finely chopped red bell peppers

¼ cup Only Sauce (page 24), plus more if needed

1 tablespoon Dijon mustard

Salt and freshly ground black pepper

¼ cup all-purpose flour

¼ cup canola or olive oil

Poached eggs

8 large eggs

2 teaspoons white vinegar

Salt and freshly ground black pepper

Cheater's hollandaise

2 cups (4 sticks) unsalted butter

6 large egg yolks

2 tablespoons heavy cream

1 tablespoon Only Rub (page 22)

2 teaspoons fresh lemon juice

Make the pork cakes: Preheat the oven to 200°F.

In a large bowl, gently mix together the pulled pork, cracker crumbs, eggs, bell peppers, sauce, mustard, 1 teaspoon salt, and ¼ teaspoon black pepper. Form the mixture into 8 patties, adding a little extra sauce if needed to help the mixture hold together.

Place the flour in a shallow dish and season with salt and pepper. Dredge the patties in the flour and shake off any excess. Heat the canola oil in a large nonstick skillet over medium heat. Cook the patties for about 5 minutes per side, or until golden brown. Transfer the cooked pork cakes to a platter and keep warm in the oven until ready to serve.

Make the poached eggs: Fill a large saucepan two-thirds full with water. Add the vinegar and bring to a boil. Break each egg into a cup or small bowl and slide them into the water one at a time. Reduce the heat to maintain a bare simmer. Poach the eggs until the whites are set but the yolks are still soft, about 3 minutes. Remove with a slotted spoon and drain on paper towels. Sprinkle with salt and pepper.

While the eggs are poaching, make the cheater's hollandaise: Melt the butter until bubbly in a small pan or in the microwave. Remove from the heat before the butter browns and set aside.

In a blender or large food processor, blend the egg yolks, heavy cream, and rub until smooth. Add half of the hot butter in a thin steady stream, slow enough so that it blends in at least as fast as you are pouring it in. Blend in the lemon juice in the same fashion, followed by the remaining butter.

Assemble the Benedicts: Divide the pulled pork cakes among serving plates. Top each with a poached egg. Drizzle with the hollandaise sauce and serve immediately.

Grilled Egg "Muffins"

This is a barbecue guy's version of the old "toad-in-the-hole," or whatever you want to call a piece of bread with an egg fried in the center of it. You can't make that on a grill, but you can crack some eggs into a muffin pan and set that pan on the grill, and your eggs will puff up into tidy little muffins that you can eat however you'd like. You can make mini-omelets by cracking the eggs in a bowl and stirring them together lightly to combine with your favorite fillings (I like shredded cheese and leftover pulled pork, personally), and then just divide the omelet mixture evenly among the muffin cups and grill them. After you've cooked these egg muffins, you can serve them in English muffins (with sausage and cheese; see below), slide them on top of lunch-type salads, and even put on top of split baked potatoes or sweet potatoes topped with a little butter, salt, and pepper.

Serves 6

Cooking spray
1 dozen eggs
1 teaspoon Only Rub (page 22)
Buttered toast for serving
Backyard Bacon (page 186) for serving, optional

Heat a charcoal grill (see page 4) or gas grill (see page 5) to medium-high heat.

Spray the holes of a 12-hole muffin pan with cooking spray and crack an egg into each hole. Sprinkle a little rub onto each egg.

Place the muffin pan on the grill and grill uncovered for 2 to 5 minutes, to desired doneness. Remove from the grill and, using a rubber spatula, gently slide the baked eggs out of the muffin pan and onto plates. Serve immediately with buttered toast and Backyard Bacon if you like.

Make it in the oven: Preheat the oven to 350°F. Crack the eggs into the muffin pan as directed above. Place the muffin pan in the oven and bake for about 15 minutes to set. If the eggs aren't cooked to your liking, return them to the oven and check about every 3 minutes until they are done.

EGG MUFFINS ON MUFFINS

When you slide the muffin pan onto the grill, also slide on some lightly buttered English muffins and breakfast sausage patties. Then make a sandwich by combining a couple of the egg "muffins" on the English muffin with a sausage patty and a slice of cheese if you like (I like pepper Jack, but sharp cheddar would be good too). Hot sauce on the side, please.

Backyard Bacon

Smoked bacon is an old German and Polish tradition, but pitmasters have known about it forever too. Bacon sold commercially in grocery stores has already been smoked, of course. But German butchers like to take raw pork belly, cure it themselves, and then smoke it for a good long while. They might smoke their bacon for twenty-four hours or more, but this book is called *Everyday Barbecue,* so let's say you don't have time to bother with all that extra curing and smoking time. I'm going to give you a shortcut to approximate the same effect if you just don't have the time. (Note: You can easily substitute store-bought cured and dried bacon in any recipe if you don't have the inclination to cure it yourself.)

Serves 4 to 6

1 tablespoon Only Rub (page 22)
1 tablespoon sugar
1 pound fresh pork belly

In a small bowl, combine the rub and sugar. Evenly coat the pork belly with the rub mixture on all sides, pressing it in to ensure that it adheres.

Place the pork belly in a large zip-top bag. Press out as much air as possible, seal the bag, and refrigerate for a week. (Massage the bag once a day or so to redistribute the cure liquid.)

After a week, the pork belly should be entirely firm in texture (if there are some soft spots, give it an extra day or two). When pork belly is fully cured, remove it from the bag, rinse it thoroughly under cold water, and pat it dry with paper towels. Discard the bag.

Prepare a smoker with soaked wood chips and heat it to 225°F (see page 6). Alternatively, prepare a charcoal grill (see page 7) or gas grill (see page 8) for smoking and heat it to medium-low heat. Allow the heat in the smoker to reduce naturally to 150°F.

Lay the pork belly in an aluminum pan.

Place the pan in the smoker and close the lid. Smoke the bacon for about 45 minutes, or until it reaches an internal temperature of 150 to 155°F. Remove the bacon from the smoker and cool on a rack. At this point the bacon is fully cooked, and you can slice it and eat it as is. Or you can fry it at a low temperature; it will not shrink as much as store-bought cured bacon.

Grilled Egg-Stuffed Peppers

Stuffed peppers is a classic dinner dish. My brunch version includes eggs and adds a touch of smoky flavor. I fill pepper halves with an omelet mixture and throw them on the grill; the peppers make a nifty little edible basket. (If you don't want to make this on the grill, you can easily do it indoors in a grill pan following the same method.)

Serves 4

2 large red bell peppers
6 large eggs
¼ cup whole milk, cream, or sour cream
¼ cup grated Parmesan cheese
Kosher salt and freshly ground black pepper
1 tablespoon Only Rub (page 22)
Buttered toast for serving, optional
Backyard Bacon (page 186) for serving, optional

Heat a charcoal grill (see page 4) or gas grill (see page 5) to medium-low heat, or pre-heat a grill pan over medium-low heat.

Cut the bell peppers in half lengthwise, making sure that the halves will lay as upright as possible on a grill with the cut sides face up. Using a spoon or sharp paring knife, clean out the insides, remove the seeds and membranes, and discard.

In a large bowl, whisk the eggs with the milk, cheese, salt and black pepper to taste, and the rub. Carefully pour the egg mixture into the pepper shells, leaving at least ¼ inch to ½ inch of room at the top.

Gently place the filled peppers on the grill, and close the top of the grill or cover the pan. Cook until the egg mixture sets and puffs up slightly, about 25 minutes. Serve warm with buttered toast and Backyard Bacon if you like.

Smoky Bacon Bloody Mary

I don't care much for fancy cocktails; Crown Royal and water suits me just fine—even at brunch. But not everyone is like me, and there are a lot of people who imbibe nothing more than a Bloody Mary before nighttime. And there is no better way to make one than this.

Note: Most of the recipes in this book require very little prep time, but for this one you're going to have to make the vodka a couple of days before you're going to use it, so plan accordingly. It's worth it.

Makes 2 large strong cocktails, plus extra bacon vodka

Bacon vodka

3 to 4 strips cured bacon
1 liter vodka

Cocktails

3 ounces bacon vodka
8 ounces good-quality tomato juice, V8 juice, or Clamato juice
2 teaspoons Worcestershire sauce
2 to 4 dashes of Louisiana-style hot sauce
Juice of 1 lemon
1 teaspoon prepared horseradish
1 teaspoon Only Rub (page 22)

Make the bacon vodka: Cook the bacon in a large cast-iron skillet over medium heat. Drain the bacon of excess grease on paper towels. Place the bacon strips directly into the vodka; if they crumble, it's fine. Seal the vodka and freeze it for 48 hours. Strain the vodka through a fine-mesh strainer; repeat straining as necessary until there are

continued

no solids in the vodka. Store the vodka in the refrigerator, straining as needed for future cocktails.

Make the cocktails: Pour all the ingredients into a large shaker and shake vigorously to combine. Strain and serve in a chilled cocktail glass with your favorite garnish. I like a big celery stalk, some pickled okra, and maybe a slice of freshly fried bacon.

Smoky Bacon Dry and Dirty Vodka Martinis

Bacon and olives aren't often seen together, but they ought to be better friends; they're both salty and savory and very good with cocktails. To my mind vodka martinis need plenty of olive juice in them, and if you insist you can pass the vermouth over the glass too. I don't usually, but you can.

Makes 2 large cocktails

1 cup very well chilled bacon vodka (page 189)
4 large pimiento-stuffed olives
2 tablespoons juice from the olive jar

Pour ½ cup vodka into each of 2 chilled martini glasses. Add 2 olives and 1 tablespoon olive juice to each glass and serve.

Grilled Honey-Vanilla French Toast

French toast is comfort food at its best. There's nothing wrong with the typical way it's done, but mine is a bit different. I cook the slices on the grill, and honey and vanilla are my not-so-secret ingredients.

Serves 3 to 6

3 large eggs
¾ cup milk
1 tablespoon honey
1 teaspoon ground cinnamon
1 teaspoon pure vanilla extract
2 tablespoons sugar
Six ¾-inch-thick slices day-old crusty bread, such as Italian bread, challah, or brioche
Favorite toppings such as whipped cream, fresh blueberries, and maple syrup

Heat a charcoal grill (see page 4) or gas grill (see page 5) to medium heat.

In a shallow bowl, whisk together the eggs, milk, honey, cinnamon, vanilla, and sugar. Coat each slice of bread on both sides with the egg mixture. Place the coated bread slices on the hot oiled grill and cook uncovered for 3 to 4 minutes per side, until browned. Serve with your favorite toppings.

Make it on the stovetop: Prepare the bread slices as directed above. Melt 2 to 3 tablespoons butter on a griddle over medium-high heat. Place the bread on the grill and press it gently with a spatula so the surface is in contact with the butter. Cover and cook for 5 to 7 minutes on the first side, until golden, then flip until golden on the other side, about 4 minutes.

Blueberry-Buttermilk Swirl Grilled Coffee Cake

Yes, I think you should make this for brunch, but a good coffee cake is a useful thing to have around for fast weekday breakfasts, after-school snacks, and weeknight desserts. So if you're turning on your grill to cook dinner anyway, you might as well slide one of these bad boys on there too. That way you'll have it for a quick brunch the next day—or for any other time you wish.

Serves 10 to 12

¾ cup (1½ sticks) unsalted butter, softened
3 cups all-purpose flour
1 tablespoon baking powder
1 teaspoon salt
1⅓ cups sugar
3 large eggs
2 teaspoons vanilla extract
¾ cup buttermilk
2 cups fresh or frozen blueberries
Powdered sugar for serving

Heat a charcoal grill (see page 4) or gas grill (see page 5) to medium heat. Generously grease a 10-cup Bundt pan with 1 tablespoon of the butter, flour it, and set aside.

In a medium bowl, whisk the flour, baking powder, and salt. In a large bowl using an electric mixer, beat the sugar and remaining butter until light and fluffy. Beat in the eggs one at a time. Beat in the vanilla. Beat in one third of the dry ingredients, followed by half of the buttermilk; repeat with a second third of the dry ingredients and the remaining half of the buttermilk; finish with the remaining third of the dry ingredients. Fold in the blueberries. Scrape the batter into the prepared pan and smooth the surface.

continued

Place the cake pan on the grill, close the lid, and cook for about 1 hour, until a skewer inserted in the center comes out clean. Remove from the grill and cool the cake in the pan on a wire rack for 10 minutes. Turn the cake out onto the rack and cool completely. (You can make the cake up to 1 day ahead; wrap it in plastic and store at room temperature.) Transfer the cake to a plate, sift powdered sugar over it, and serve.

Make it in the oven: Preheat the oven to 350°F. Prepare the pan and batter as directed above. After the batter is poured into the pan, bake until a tester inserted near the center of cake comes out clean, about 1 hour. Remove from the oven and cool the cake in the pan on a wire rack for 10 minutes. Turn the cake out onto the rack and cool completely. Transfer the cake to a plate, sift powdered sugar over it, and serve.

Smoked Egg Salad English Muffins

Smoking eggs gives them a lot of character and a very deep intensity. You can smoke these and eat them as is, sprinkled with a little salt, pepper, and Only Rub (page 22), but they're better when you blend them into this unforgettable egg salad, piled onto toasted English muffins.

Makes 16 sandwiches

12 large eggs

Kosher salt

1 large stalk celery, finely diced

½ cup mayonnaise

¼ cup sour cream

2 teaspoons fresh lemon juice,
  or more to taste

2 teaspoons Dijon mustard

Freshly ground black pepper

1 tablespoon Only Rub (page 22)

16 English muffins, split and well toasted

4 tablespoons (½ stick) unsalted butter,
  softened

Place the eggs in a large, heavy stockpot and add water to cover. Add 1 tablespoon salt and bring to a boil over high heat. Remove the pot from the heat and cover it. Leave the eggs to continue cooking in the covered pot for 10 minutes, then drain. Cover the eggs with ice-cold water. When cool enough to handle, peel them under cold running water.

Prepare a smoker with soaked wood chips and heat it to 225°F (see page 6). Alternatively, prepare a charcoal grill (see page 7) or gas grill (see page 8) for smoking and heat it to medium-low heat. Lightly oil a cast-iron grill pan.

Arrange the eggs in the prepared cast-iron grill pan, cover, and smoke for 30 to 40 minutes, until the eggs develop a light brown color from the smoke. Transfer the eggs to a plate and let them cool off until cool enough to handle, about 10 minutes. Dice the eggs and place them in a large bowl. Add the celery, mayonnaise, sour cream, lemon juice, mustard, salt and pepper to taste, and rub, and stir to gently combine. (The egg salad may be made ahead to this point and refrigerated overnight.)

Spread the toasted English muffin halves with the softened butter and arrange them on a work surface. Spoon the egg salad over eight of the slices, close the sandwiches with the remaining slices, and cut them in half. Serve immediately.

nine

LEFTOVERS

BABY BACK MAC AND CHEESE

BARBECUE EGGROLLS

BARBECUE BRISKET POTATO SOUP

BARBECUE BRISKET CHILI

BOSS COBB SALAD

BARBECUE STUFFED MUSHROOMS

BARBECUE CHICKEN AND EGG SALAD WITH BACON

BARBECUE PASTA SALAD

BARBECUE PORK AND BLACK BEAN BURRITOS

TINGA-STYLE BARBECUE TACOS

BARBECUE BURNT END WRAPS

PULLED PORK BURGERS

BARBECUE PIZZA

BARBECUE CHICKEN CAKES

BARBECUE PORK AND MASHED POTATO PIE

After my first book, *Smokin' with Myron Mixon,* came out, a lot of people got to see and taste the food I cook when I win national barbecue competitions. That's my day job and I'm damn good at it, and here's hoping you're good at yours too. A lot of people come up to me at festivals and ask about what I eat when I'm *not* working. And I usually laugh and explain that the thing I eat the most of is leftovers.

I'm passionate about leftovers because I hate to waste good food, and we've got a big problem in this country with doing just that. I think cooks in the old days, even as recently as the fifties and sixties, were much better than we are today at repurposing leftovers and knowing not only how to stretch a dollar into a meal, but how to stretch one meal into two. Knowing what to do with leftovers involves creativity and ingenuity, and it's becoming a lost art. If you spend any time at a smoker, you're most likely cooking up a whole lot of meat—way more than you and your family could eat in one sitting, no matter how great it is. That's a good thing: It means that you have several more delicious meals in your future, and this chapter will introduce you to some of my favorites.

"But what if I don't have leftovers?" you might ask me. And I'd look at you real funny, because who eats every last bite of everything he or she cooks? Probably not you, and I know for sure not me. Let's apply some common sense to this problem. Say you got yourself a smoker and you want to make my Barbecue Whole Chicken the Easy Way (page 33) for dinner. (Great idea, by the way, especially on a busy weeknight.) The best advice I can give you is to make two of those suckers, and that way you'll have dinner that night and then enough leftovers for a Boss Cobb Salad (page 212), sandwiches with Barbecue Chicken and Egg Salad with Bacon (page 214), and a Barbecue Pizza (page 224). Planning to have leftovers and knowing what to do with them—that's how you're going to solve the age-old problem of dinner on a busy weeknight. And now you get to solve it with barbecue. Magic.

Baby Back Mac and Cheese

Home-style macaroni and cheese should be rich and thick and gooey, and oven-baked so that it holds together. I'm not messing around with the stovetop version; I'm talking about a huge casserole that can feed a crowd and keep it filled up. Now, there are plenty of versions of mac and cheese that add tasty bits of bacon, which is a nice little touch. But I don't take any half steps. My version calls for smoky, juicy baby back rib meat that doesn't melt into the background. It stands up to the macaroni and cheese and carries this all-time favorite to new heights. Just ask anyone who's had it at my Pride and Joy Bar B Que spots.

Serves 4 for a main course or 8 for a side dish

4 tablespoons (½ stick) unsalted butter, softened
Salt
1 pound elbow macaroni
2 tablespoons all-purpose flour
3 cups milk
2½ cups shredded sharp cheddar cheese
Freshly ground black pepper
1 pound leftover baby back rib meat (leftover pulled pork, brisket, or pulled chicken
    would work, too)

Generously butter a 13 x 9-inch baking pan on the bottom and sides with 2 table-spoons of the butter.

Bring a large pot of salted water to a boil over high heat. Add the macaroni and cook to al dente according to the package directions.

Once you drop the pasta into the water, melt the remaining 2 tablespoons butter in a medium saucepan over medium-high heat. Sprinkle the flour over the melted butter and cook, stirring, for about 1 minute, until the butter and flour form a paste that is beginning to slightly brown. Slowly whisk in the milk and bring the mixture up to a

continued

bubble to thicken. Remove the saucepan from the heat, whisk in 2 cups of the shredded cheese, and season with salt and pepper.

Preheat the broiler.

Drain the macaroni and return it to the pot it was cooked in. Add the cheese sauce and stir in the leftover rib meat. Pour the baby back mac into the prepared baking pan and scatter the top with the remaining ½ cup cheese. Put it in the broiler and broil until the cheese is golden brown on top, 3 to 4 minutes. Remove from the broiler and let stand, covered with foil, for 15 minutes before serving.

Barbecue Eggrolls

Where I live in Unadilla, almost in the very middle of the great state of Georgia, there are not a whole lot of what you might call authentic Chinese restaurants. But we do have some places that serve the beloved Americanized versions of Chinese dishes that so many of us were first introduced to and have an enduring soft spot for—like eggrolls. My eggrolls make for great party food, with barbecue sauce on the side instead of the usual duck sauce. And these are baked, so they're not nearly as greasy as the take-out kind.

Makes 12 eggrolls

3 tablespoons extra-virgin olive oil

¾ pound leftover barbecue, such as
 pulled pork, chopped

1 onion, chopped

2 bell peppers, cored, seeded,
 and chopped

Salt and freshly ground black pepper

2 tablespoons Worcestershire sauce

12 egg roll wrappers

Cooking spray

Barbecue sauce for serving

Preheat the oven to 375°F.

Heat the olive oil in a large skillet over medium-high heat. Add the leftover barbecue and brown it thoroughly, about 5 minutes. Add the onions and bell peppers to the pan and season with salt and pepper. Cook for about 5 minutes, until the onions are softened. Mix in the Worcestershire sauce, then remove from the heat and set aside to cool.

To wrap the egg rolls, set a wire rack on top of a baking sheet and fill a small bowl with water. Brush water around all four sides of a wrapper to act as the glue. Place ¼ cup of the meat mixture in the center of the wrapper. Fold two corners into the center, then fold one of the remaining corners over the filling and roll toward the last corner, creating a long skinny roll. Place the finished rolls on the sheet pan with the wire rack and repeat with the remaining wrappers and filling.

Coat the egg rolls with cooking spray, place in the oven, and bake for 20 to 25 minutes, until browned. Serve immediately, with barbecue sauce on the side for dipping.

Barbecue Brisket Potato Soup

This is what I want to eat for dinner on a Monday night in late January, when it's cold outside and I don't feel like having to work too hard to get dinner on the table. I want something hearty, something familiar, and something that's going to fill me up. This soup does the trick every time. The soup can be refrigerated for up to 2 days; reheat gently.

Serves 4

2 tablespoons olive oil
4 leeks, green parts removed and discarded, white parts cleaned and chopped
4 to 5 garlic cloves, chopped
2 teaspoons dried thyme
1 tablespoon paprika, plus more for garnish
Salt and freshly ground black pepper
4 pounds russet potatoes, peeled and chopped
1½ quarts chicken stock
1 pound leftover brisket, chopped
A dash of hot sauce, optional
1 cup shredded sharp cheddar cheese
1 cup shredded Parmesan cheese
Chopped scallions for garnish
Sour cream for garnish, optional
Paprika, optional

Heat the olive oil in a large, heavy-bottomed saucepan over medium-high heat. Add the leeks and garlic and sauté until the leeks are softened, 4 to 5 minutes. Add the thyme and paprika and season with salt and pepper. Add the potatoes and stock and bring to boil. Reduce the heat to medium and simmer until the potatoes are cooked through, 8 to 10 minutes. Puree the soup until smooth using a blender, food processor, or immersion blender.

Return the soup to the pan if you removed it to blend and add the leftover brisket. Adjust the seasonings as needed with salt, pepper, and hot sauce, if using. Bring the soup back up to a boil, then immediately remove it from the heat. Serve the soup in bowls or mugs topped with some of the 2 cheeses, a sprinkling of scallions, a dollop of sour cream, and a dash of paprika if you like.

Barbecue Brisket Chili

I'm not from Texas, which is my way of saying that the word "chili" conjures up a con-coction of ground beef *and* beans. If you take that basic formula but substitute leftover brisket, you get a hybrid chili that's the best of both worlds: It has the toothsome meatiness of Texas chili and the full meal appeal of the ground beef-and-beans ver-sion that I grew up loving.

Serves 10 to 12

¼ cup olive oil
2 cups chopped yellow onions
6 large garlic cloves, minced
2 tablespoons chili powder
1 tablespoon crushed red pepper flakes
1 tablespoon cayenne pepper, or to taste
2 tablespoons ground cumin
2 green bell peppers, cored, seeded, and diced
1 bay leaf
6 cups chopped tomatoes with their liquid
5 pounds leftover barbecue brisket
Salt and freshly ground black pepper
½ cup beer, preferably lager
Two 15-ounce cans red kidney beans
Sour cream and grated cheddar cheese for serving

Heat the olive oil in a very large, heavy-bottomed saucepan over medium heat. Add the onions and garlic and sauté until softened but not browned, 8 to 10 minutes. Add the chili powder, red pepper flakes, cayenne, and cumin and sauté for about 1 minute. Add the bell peppers, bay leaf, tomatoes with their juice, the leftover barbecue brisket, 1 tablespoon salt, and 1 teaspoon pepper and bring to a boil. Reduce the heat to low, cover the pot with a tight-fitting lid, and simmer for about 2½ hours, stirring occasionally. Add the beer, cover the pan, and simmer for about 1 more hour.

Add the kidney beans and heat to warm through. Taste and season with salt if needed. Transfer the chili to serving bowls and serve with sour cream and grated cheddar on the side.

Boss Cobb Salad

Bet you didn't know that the Cobb salad was invented in the 1930s by restaurateur Robert Cobb at his Brown Derby restaurant in Los Angeles during the Hollywood studio system heyday. The inspiration? A host of leftovers Cobb allegedly had hanging around in the restaurant's kitchen. Here's my version of the same. What's great about a Cobb salad is that you can organize each bite however you like by picking and choosing among the rows of composed ingredients.

Serves 4 as a main course

1 large head romaine lettuce, chopped into bite-size pieces

¾ to 1 pound diced leftover barbecue chicken, pork, or brisket (about 2 cups)

8 slices crisp cooked bacon, crumbled

3 hard-boiled eggs, chopped

2 tomatoes, diced

1 Hass avocado, diced

¼ pound blue cheese, crumbled

8 chives, chopped, optional

1 small garlic clove, minced

1 teaspoon Dijon mustard

1 tablespoon mayonnaise

1 teaspoon Worcestershire sauce

1 tablespoon fresh lemon juice

⅓ cup red wine vinegar

¼ cup extra-virgin olive oil

¼ cup canola oil

Salt and freshly ground black pepper

Divide the lettuce among 4 large plates.

Assemble the salad: Arrange the leftover barbecue chicken, bacon, eggs, tomatoes, avocados, and blue cheese in that order in decorative rows atop the lettuce. Sprinkle chopped chives over the top, if using.

Make the dressing: In a blender, combine the garlic, mustard, mayonnaise, Worcestershire sauce, lemon juice, vinegar, and olive oil and blend until smooth. With the machine on, gradually drizzle in the canola oil until the dressing is emulsified. Season with salt and pepper.

Serve the salad and pass the dressing in a gravy boat.

Barbecue Stuffed Mushrooms

Everybody loves stuffed mushrooms because everybody loves food that's easy to pick up and pop into your mouth. They will be delicious with any leftover meat you have around; the best way to serve them is piping hot, fresh out of the oven. (Save those mushroom stems and use to flavor stocks and stews.)

Serves 4 as an appetizer

6 tablespoons unsalted butter
1 shallot, minced
Kosher salt
1 cup finely chopped leftover barbecue meat, such as pulled pork or pulled chicken
⅓ cup heavy cream
2 teaspoons fresh lemon juice
¼ cup water
1 pound large white mushrooms caps
1 tablespoon chopped scallions

Melt 4 tablespoons of the butter in a medium skillet over low heat. Add the shallot and a pinch of salt, cover, and cook until softened, about 2 minutes. Add the leftover barbecue meat, increase the heat to medium-low, and warm the meat through, about 5 minutes. Add the cream and lemon juice, cover partially, and cook until the mixture is slightly thickened, about 5 minutes.

Pour the water into a large skillet. Add the remaining 2 tablespoons butter and a generous pinch of salt and bring to a boil over high heat. Add the mushroom caps, stemmed side up, reduce the heat to medium, cover, and cook until softened but still firm enough to be stuffed, about 5 minutes. Uncover and cook, stirring occasionally, until the liquid has evaporated and the caps are browned, about 5 minutes longer. Turn the caps stemmed side down to drain any remaining liquid.

Transfer the caps to a platter, spoon in the filling, and scatter the scallions on top. Serve while hot.

Barbecue Chicken and Egg Salad with Bacon

Here was my thinking behind this dish: I like potato salad made with eggs and bacon, and I like chicken salad. What if I get rid of the potatoes, which can take a while to cook anyway, and make chicken salad with eggs and bacon instead? It packs a huge protein wallop if you're into that, and it's also great on sandwiches or piled on top of a big bed of lightly dressed lettuce.

Serves 6

½ pound bacon, sliced
1 tablespoon Dijon mustard
2 tablespoons white vinegar
Salt and freshly ground black pepper
½ cup olive oil
½ cup mayonnaise
½ cup sour cream
3 large hard-boiled eggs, peeled
5 scallions, chopped
2 pounds leftover barbecue chicken, at room temperature

Preheat the oven to 350°F.

Line a baking sheet with foil and place a wire rack over the pan. Place the bacon on the rack, place in the oven, and bake for about 20 minutes, until crisp. Transfer to a plate lined with paper towels to drain.

In a small bowl, whisk together the mustard, vinegar, and salt and pepper to taste. Slowly whisk in the olive oil to blend, then whisk in the mayonnaise and sour cream.

Coarsely chop the hard-boiled eggs and crumble the bacon. Place them in a large bowl, add the scallions and leftover barbecue chicken, and toss to combine. Pour the dressing over the top and toss to coat. Season with salt and pepper if needed. Serve at room temperature or cover and chill for an hour and serve chilled.

Barbecue Pasta Salad

How many picnics have you been to that feature pasta salad? That's because it's good to eat and easy to make. I use ear-shaped orecchiette in this salad because I like the ridges and the way the pasta not only holds its shape but also gathers the flavors of the other ingredients in the salad.

Serves 4

Salt
1 pound orecchiette pasta
1 garlic clove, grated
1 cup chopped parsley
½ cup Only Sauce (page 24)
¼ cup red wine vinegar
¼ to ½ cup extra-virgin olive oil
Freshly ground black pepper
¼ pound thickly sliced provolone, chopped
6 jarred roasted red bell peppers, finely diced
1 large fresh red bell pepper, cored, seeded, and diced
1 red onion, finely diced
1 pound leftover barbecue pulled pork or pulled chicken

Bring a large pot of salted water to a boil over high heat. Add the pasta and cook to al dente according to the package directions. Drain and cool.

In a medium bowl, combine the garlic, parsley, sauce, and vinegar. Slowly whisk in the olive oil to emulsify into a dressing. Season with salt and black pepper.

In a large bowl, toss the pasta, dressing, chopped cheese, jarred and fresh bell peppers, onions, and leftover barbecue pork or chicken. Serve at room temperature.

Barbecue Pork and Black Bean Burritos

Everybody knows that pork and beans are two tastes that go great together, and here I'm combining them in a Mexican theme. I love burritos, not just because I like Mexican food, but also because I'm a big fan of handheld foods in general—pizza, corndogs, ribs, and the like. Burritos are also extremely easy to make, and they're good for family dinners because even the pickiest eaters you've got can fill them however they like.

Makes 4 burritos

1 pound leftover barbecue pulled pork
One 15-ounce can black beans, drained and rinsed
Salt
½ pound Monterey Jack, pepper Jack, or cheddar cheese, or a combination of
    all three, shredded (about 2 cups)
1 ripe tomato, chopped
2 tablespoons fresh lime juice (from about 1 lime)
1 red onion, chopped
Four 9-inch flour tortillas
Sour cream, salsa, and lime wedges for serving

Preheat the oven to 350°F.

In a large skillet, reheat the leftover barbecue pulled pork over medium heat, breaking it up with a fork or wooden spoon, until cooked through and just beginning to brown, about 5 minutes. Remove from the heat.

Pour off all but 1 tablespoon fat from the pan and reduce the heat to low. Add the beans, season with salt, and cook, mashing the beans with the back of a wooden spoon, until heated through, 2 to 3 minutes. Most of the beans should be broken up, but don't mash them to a puree. Remove from the heat and stir in half of the cheese, the tomatoes, lime juice, and onions.

Spread one quarter of the bean mixture in a line just below the center of each tortilla. Sprinkle the remaining cheese on top of the beans. Roll up the burritos and place them seam side down in a small baking dish. Bake until the cheese is melted and the filling is hot, about 15 minutes. If the tops begin to brown too much, cover loosely with aluminum foil. Serve immediately, with sour cream, your favorite salsa, and lime wedges on the side.

Tinga-Style Barbecue Tacos

Classic Mexican tinga is pork in a smoky tomato-based sauce. (The word "tinga" refers to "torn" pieces of meat, not unlike the way we hand shred barbecue sometimes.) There are countless formulas for how to make it. In Mexico it involves smoking the tomatoes; for me, knee-deep in Southern barbecue territory, it involves smoking the pork.

Serves 6

2 tablespoons olive oil

1 large onion, thinly sliced

Salt and freshly ground black pepper

3 large garlic cloves, minced

One 28-ounce can diced tomatoes with juices

1 tablespoon steak sauce

1 teaspoon Louisiana-style hot sauce

1 cup chicken stock

2 pounds leftover barbecue pulled pork or barbecue chicken

24 corn tortillas

2 ounces shredded sharp cheddar, Monterey Jack, or pepper Jack cheese

2 cups shredded iceberg lettuce for serving, optional

1 cup sour cream for serving, optional

Heat the olive oil in a large nonstick skillet over medium-high heat. Add the onions, season with salt and pepper, and cook, stirring occasionally, until lightly browned and softened, about 5 minutes. Add the garlic and cook for 2 minutes more. Add the tomatoes and their juices, the steak sauce, hot sauce, and stock and bring to a boil. Reduce the heat to medium and simmer, stirring occasionally, until thickened and slightly reduced, about 20 minutes.

Add the leftover barbecue pulled pork or chicken to the sauce and stir to reheat it in the sauce, about 5 minutes. Spoon about 3 tablespoons of the meat-and-onion mixture onto each tortilla and sprinkle with the shredded cheese. Serve the tacos with the shredded lettuce and sour cream if you like.

Barbecue Brisket Wraps

Folks like to eat foods that they can hold on to—and I especially love wraps, they're so easy to handle. These particular ones are delicious, a cross between a taco, with the thinly sliced peppers and onion, and a classic brisket sandwich. Combinations like this one are what "everyday barbecue" is all about: Taking what you've got and making the most of it, so you can have a little bit of barbecue whenever you please.

Makes about 3 dozen appetizer-size wraps

1 tablespoon olive oil
2 green or red or combination bell peppers, cored, seeded, and cut into 2-inch-long
    strips
1 medium onion, thinly sliced
1 tablespoon cider vinegar
2 teaspoons Only Rub (page 22)
Salt and freshly ground black pepper
1 pound leftover burnt brisket ends
Six 8-inch flour tortillas
⅓ cup mayonnaise
12 lettuce leaves
6 tablespoons Only Sauce (page 24)

Heat the olive oil in a large skillet over medium heat. Add the bell peppers and onions and cook, stirring, until softened and browned, about 10 minutes. Add the vinegar and rub and cook until the vinegar evaporates, about 2 minutes. Season with salt and pepper.

Preheat the broiler and position a rack 8 inches from the heat. Season the leftover brisket with salt and black pepper, place on a baking sheet, and broil for about 2 minutes per side, until the brisket is sizzling and deep mahogany. Transfer the brisket to a cutting board, cover loosely with foil, and let stand for 5 minutes. Thinly slice the ends against the grain.

Spread a tortilla with a thin layer of mayonnaise and top with 2 to 3 slices of burnt ends in a single layer. Season with salt and black pepper, then add 2 lettuce leaves and spread 1 tablespoon of the sauce along the lettuce. Roll up the tortilla and seal the roll with a little mayonnaise if necessary. Cut off the ends to make a neat roll and set aside on a platter if you're planning to serve or a cutting board if you're planning to slice first. Repeat with the remaining tortillas and filling. Slice the rolls 1 inch thick, secure with a toothpick through the center if you like, and serve.

Pulled Pork Burgers

Some people may call topping a burger with pulled pork gilding the lily, but who needs them? I call it taking your burger to the next level. Here's how.

Makes 4 to 6 burgers

1½ pounds ground beef, preferably ground chuck with at least 20% fat, at room temperature
2 teaspoons Dijon mustard
1 tablespoon Only Rub (page 22)
Salt and freshly ground black pepper
4 to 6 hamburger buns, split
2 tablespoons unsalted butter, melted
12 ounces leftover pulled pork, reheated
4 to 6 tablespoons Only Sauce (page 24)
Lettuce, tomato, and any other toppings you like

Heat a charcoal grill (see page 4) or gas grill (see page 5) to medium-high heat.

In a medium bowl, combine the beef with the mustard and rub, gently kneading into 4 to 6 equal patties, about ¾ inch thick each. Season the burgers very generously with salt and pepper and transfer to a plate lined with plastic wrap.

Grill the burgers directly on the grill for about 10 minutes, turning once, for medium. Move the burgers away from the heat to rest on a warm (but definitely not hot) part of the grill. Brush the cut sides of the buns with the melted butter and grill the cut sides of the buns for about 1 minute, until toasted.

Slide the burgers onto the buns and finish them by topping each with a small handful of pulled pork and Only Sauce, plus lettuce and tomato and whatever toppings you prefer. Serve immediately.

Barbecue Pizza

Here's what to do: Go to your favorite pizzeria, tell them you want to make some pizza at home, and ask them to sell you some dough. For about $2, I can get 1 pound from my local joint. Top that with leftover barbecue, stick it in the oven, and, I'm telling you, the cost of a delicious weeknight dinner just went down substantially. (And if you're in a very serious pinch, you can depend on the rolled-up pie crust dough next to the crescent rolls in the grocery store refrigerator section. Everybody has an emergency sometime.)

Serves 6 to 8

2 cups leftover barbecue chicken or barbecue pork, shredded
1 medium red onion, thinly sliced
¾ cup Only Sauce (page 24)
½ pound Monterey Jack cheese, shredded (about 2 cups)
1 pound store-bought pizza dough, at room temperature
1 teaspoon extra-virgin olive oil
Salt and freshly ground black pepper

Preheat a pizza stone in a 500°F oven. Alternatively, generously oil a baking sheet.

In a medium bowl, combine the leftover barbecue, onions, sauce, and half of the cheese. Set aside.

On a lightly floured surface, roll or stretch the dough to a rough 14-inch round. Transfer the dough to a floured pizza peel or rimless cookie sheet, or directly to the oiled baking sheet. Spread the barbecue-and-onion mixture on the pizza, leaving a 1-inch border of dough. Brush the border with the olive oil, sprinkle the remaining cheese over the top, and season with salt and pepper.

Slide the pizza onto the hot stone, if using, and bake for about 10 minutes on the stone or 16 minutes on the baking sheet, until the crust is golden and the cheese is bubbling. Transfer the pizza to a wire rack and cool slightly before serving.

Barbecue Chicken Cakes

Maryland may have its crab cakes, but here in middle Georgia, where barbecue reigns supreme, we have our chicken cakes. It's the same idea, only instead of using fresh crab and oyster crackers to make our cakes, we use leftover barbecue chicken and Ritz crackers. You should eat these any way you would the crab version. They are very good in a sandwich with some slaw, or in a fancier presentation atop mashed potatoes or polenta.

Makes 8 chicken cakes; serves 4

½ cup finely crushed Ritz crackers
1 large egg
2 tablespoons milk
2 tablespoons grated Parmesan cheese
½ teaspoon garlic salt
2 cups finely chopped leftover barbecue chicken
¼ cup vegetable oil
1 recipe Only Slaw (page 37) for serving, optional
1½ cups Only Sauce (page 24)

In medium bowl, combine the crackers, egg, milk, cheese, and garlic salt. Stir in the leftover barbecue chicken.

Shape the chicken mixture into eight 3-inch cakes using about ¼ cup for each.

Heat the vegetable oil in a 12-inch nonstick skillet over medium-high heat. Fry the cakes for 4 to 5 minutes, turning once, until golden brown. Remove from the skillet and drain on paper towels.

Serve the cakes immediately, topped with slaw, if using, and a side of sauce.

Barbecue Pork and Mashed Potato Pie

This is a Southerner's shepherd's pie, made with leftover barbecue and freshly mashed potatoes. Serve it with a salad and some bread and you've got the idea of "everyday barbecue" right in your kitchen. It's so easy and so much better than whatever else you thought you'd cook for dinner after soccer practice or a long day at the office.

Serves 6

2 pounds Yukon gold potatoes, peeled and cut into 2-inch pieces
Kosher salt
4 tablespoons olive oil
Freshly ground black pepper
1 large onion, chopped
1½ pounds leftover barbecue pulled pork
4 plum tomatoes, seeded and diced
½ cup ketchup
2 tablespoons cider vinegar
1 tablespoon Dijon mustard
1 tablespoon molasses
1 tablespoon Worcestershire sauce

Place the potatoes in a large saucepan and add cold water to cover. Bring to a boil over high heat and add 1 teaspoon salt; reduce the heat and simmer until just tender, 15 to 18 minutes. Drain the potatoes, reserving ¼ cup of the cooking liquid, and return the potatoes to the pan. Mash the potatoes with 3 tablespoons of the olive oil, ¼ teaspoon salt, ¼ teaspoon pepper, and 2 tablespoons of the reserved cooking liquid; add more liquid if necessary.

While the potatoes are cooking, heat the remaining 1 tablespoon olive oil in a large skillet over medium heat. Add the onions, ¼ teaspoon salt, and ¼ teaspoon pepper, cover, and cook, stirring occasionally, until softened, 8 to 10 minutes.

Preheat the broiler.

Add the leftover barbecue pulled pork to the onions and cook, breaking it up with a spoon, until warmed through, about 5 minutes. Spoon off and discard any excess fat. Add the tomatoes and cook, stirring occasionally, for about 4 minutes. In a small bowl, whisk together the ketchup, vinegar, mustard, molasses, and Worcestershire sauce; add to the pork and cook, stirring, for about 1 minute.

Transfer the pork mixture to a 2-quart broiler-proof baking dish and top with the mashed potatoes. Broil until beginning to brown, 2 to 4 minutes. Serve immediately.

ten

SALADS
AND SIDES

GRILLED HICKORY-SMOKED CAPRESE SALAD

THE PITMASTER'S WEDGE

HAIL CAESAR SMOKY SALAD

WATERMELON, FETA, RED ONION, AND MINT SUMMER SALAD

SPINACH SALAD WITH PEACHES, PECANS, AND CREAMY POPPY SEED DRESSING

GRILLED HICKORY-SMOKED SUMMER SQUASH AND ZUCCHINI SALAD

MEXICAN-STYLE GRILLED CORN

SMOKED POTATOES

PITMASTER-STYLE GRILLED VEGGIE KEBABS

SMOKY COLLARD GREENS

BARBECUE JALAPEÑO-CHEDDAR HUSHPUPPIES

BARBECUE SMOKED CABBAGE

SLOW-SMOKED BARBECUE CHERRY TOMATOES

VIDALIA ONION RELISH

GRILLED SWEET ONION AND GREEN TOMATO CHOWCHOW

I t's the mark of a good cook who knows how to best showcase his smoked and grilled meats by pairing them with the right dishes, and I'm here to help you get there.

I like salads that whet the appetite for what's to come, that provide a light freshness that complements the distinct and strong flavor of smoke-kissed meat. I like side dishes that add depth and richness and new flavor profiles to a meal so that the smoked meat has something to play off of, to work with, if you will. In my first book I gave readers the classics, the side dishes we're all used to seeing with barbecue: baked beans, potato salad, creamy coleslaw (see page 37 for my updated version), and Brunswick stew. Those are staples, the kinds of sides that you expect to see at any table where barbecue is served. But those hearty—even heavy—classics aren't for everyday eating. I save them for special occasions when we want to blow it out and don't care about calories and fat. For dinner on a regular night at home, I'm giving you side dishes that are quicker and easier to prepare and a bit lighter and healthier too.

Now, the point of this book is that not only can you cook barbecue quickly, but that you can make it a little more interesting too. One of the best ways to do that is with a unique salad or side dish—like my Barbecue Smoked Cabbage (page 254), Mexican-Style Grilled Corn (page 245), and Grilled Hickory-Smoked Summer Squash and Zucchini Salad (page 243). These dishes will show you that there's more to life than baked beans. These sides and salads are quick and easy to make, and they will be game changers at your next backyard feast.

Grilled Hickory-Smoked Caprese Salad

When you put tomatoes on the smoker they become soft and succulent, bursting with tangy juices; if you add them to a classic Caprese salad with fresh mozzarella and basil leaves and drizzle a little balsamic vinegar on top, they're excellent. (Of course, I also like them served alongside brisket, and I don't even need sauce when I do it that way.)

Serves 4 as a side dish

4 large homegrown tomatoes (about 1 pound), quartered
1 pint grape or cherry tomatoes
1 pint small mixed heirloom tomatoes, cut in half if large
½ cup extra-virgin olive oil
1½ tablespoons Only Rub (page 22)
8 ounces fresh mozzarella, cut into 4 thick slices
2 cups fresh basil leaves
2 tablespoons balsamic vinegar

Heat a charcoal grill (see page 4) or gas grill (see page 5) to medium-high heat.

Arrange 4 large (about 12- by 24-inch) sheets of heavy-duty aluminum foil on a work surface. Mound a quarter of the tomatoes in the center of each sheet, drizzle with the olive oil, and season with the rub. Fold up the foil to create tight packets.

Set the packets on the grill, cover, and grill for 15 to 20 minutes, until the tomatoes begin to soften and burst. Using scissors, carefully cut open the foil packets and let the tomatoes cool to room temperature.

Meanwhile, make the salad: Lay a slice of the mozzarella on each of 4 plates and place a few basil leaves on top of each slice. Drizzle the vinegar over the basil and let it trickle onto the mozzarella. Serve immediately with the tomatoes.

The Pitmaster's Wedge

Steakhouses are deluxe restaurants where you get to sit in a clubby room, eat a big piece of perfectly cooked meat that's a little charred on the outside and tender and juicy in the middle, and drink an ice-cold whiskey. That's damn near ideal to me. And what does the meal start with? A wedge of crisp and cool iceberg garnished with freshly fried bacon and creamy dressing. So what's a pitmaster to do if he wants to make it barbecue friendly? Not a damn thing. This salad's perfect. Here's how I like to put it together with a little barbecue spin on the dressing.

Serves 4

1 teaspoon Only Rub (page 22)
½ cup sour cream
1 cup mayonnaise
2 tablespoons white wine vinegar or other mild vinegar
1 tablespoon fresh lemon juice
1 small garlic clove, smashed and minced
1 tablespoon buttermilk
2 tablespoons minced scallions
1 medium head iceberg lettuce, cut into 4 wedges
4 slices very crisp cooked bacon

Make the dressing: In a large bowl or blender, whisk or blend the rub, sour cream, mayonnaise, vinegar, lemon juice, and garlic until smooth. Add the buttermilk to thin the dressing. Stir in the scallions. Pour into a jar with a tight-fitting lid and refrigerate for a few hours to allow the flavors to combine. Shake well before using. (The dressing keeps in the refrigerator for up to 1 week.)

Make the salad: Place 1 lettuce wedge on each plate. Pour some dressing over the top and crumble 1 slice of bacon over each wedge. Serve immediately.

Hail Caesar Smoky Salad

Cooked lettuce isn't anything new. We've been stewing greens in the South since we discovered fire. As I understand it, the Caesar salad was invented in Tijuana, Mexico, and the amalgam of flavors—the essence of the sea from the anchovy, the rich saltiness of the Parmesan cheese, the bright bite of lemon—is delicious. But I got to thinking about how I could add a bit of smoke to the proceedings. Grilling the long hearty leaves of romaine is just the ticket.

Serves 8 as an appetizer or 4 as a main course

1 large egg
1½ tablespoons fresh lemon juice
1 teaspoon minced garlic
¼ teaspoon Worcestershire sauce
$1/8$ teaspoon red pepper flakes
½ tablespoon Dijon mustard
1 anchovy fillet, smashed with a fork
½ cup peanut oil
3 tablespoons plus 1 teaspoon olive oil
2 tablespoons freshly grated Parmesan cheese, plus more for serving
Salt and freshly ground black pepper
4 romaine lettuce hearts, cut in half lengthwise
1 teaspoon Only Rub (page 22)

Make the dressing: In a medium bowl, whisk together the egg, lemon juice, garlic, Worcestershire sauce, red pepper flakes, mustard, and anchovy. Whisking continuously, slowly pour in the peanut oil and 3 tablespoons olive oil to emulsify. Stir in the cheese and season with salt and pepper. Pour into a container, cover, and refrigerate. When ready to use, whisk again.

Heat a charcoal grill (see page 4) or gas grill (see page 5) to medium-high heat.

Drizzle the cut side of the romaine hearts with the remaining 1 teaspoon olive oil, and sprinkle with salt, pepper, and the rub. Grill the romaine hearts cut side down until charred in spots, about 20 seconds. Turn the romaine hearts over and grill for 20 seconds longer. Transfer to a platter cut side up.

Drizzle the dressing over the romaine, sprinkle with more cheese, and serve immediately. Refrigerate any leftover dressing; it will keep, refrigerated, for up to 2 weeks.

Watermelon, Feta, Red Onion, and Mint Summer Salad

Juicy watermelon is one of the best parts of summer, and there's absolutely nothing wrong with hunkering down with a slice or two or three at a backyard barbecue. What's neat about watermelon, though, is its combination of sweetness and crunch, which is great in a salad. I toss cubes of it with some sweet onion, a little mint, and a handful of creamy feta, and it's so light and refreshing that it makes me want to eat some barbecue.

Serves 4 as an appetizer

¼ cup extra-virgin olive oil
1½ tablespoons fresh lemon juice
½ teaspoon Louisiana-style hot sauce
Salt and freshly ground black pepper
1½ pounds seedless watermelon, rind removed, fruit cubed ¼ inch thick
¼ small red onion, thinly sliced
¼ cup coarsely chopped mint
2 ounces feta cheese, crumbled (about ½ cup)

In a small bowl, whisk the olive oil with the lemon juice and hot sauce and season with salt and pepper. Arrange the watermelon cubes on a platter and sprinkle with the onions, mint, and feta. Drizzle the dressing on top and serve immediately.

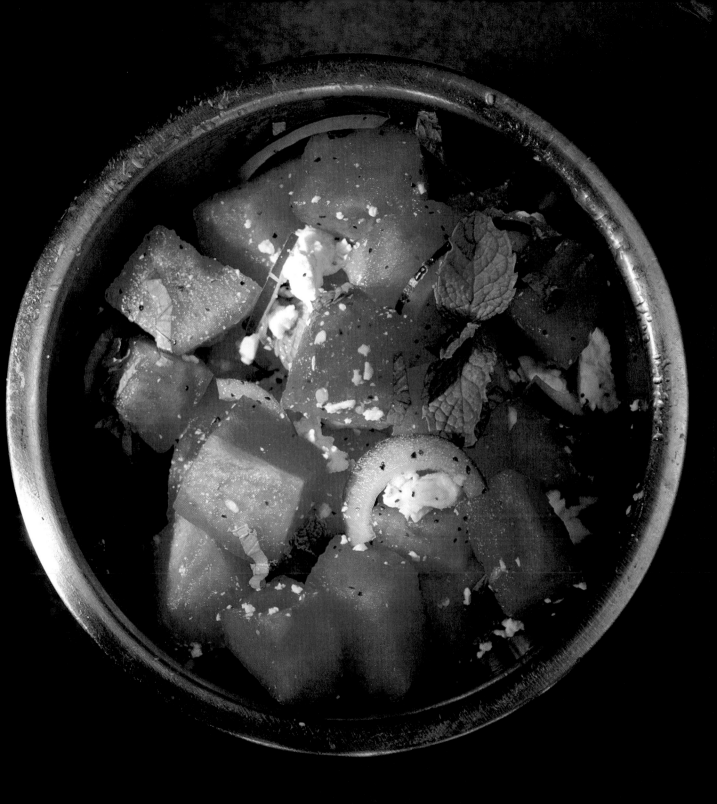

Spinach Salad with Peaches, Pecans, and Creamy Poppy Seed Dressing

Like all good Georgians, I love the combination of our rich, intense pecans with the delicate and fragrant subtlety of ripe peaches. What ties this Southern take on spinach salad together, though, is the creamy poppy seed dressing, which is simultaneously tangy and sweet, a killer combination.

Serves 2 as entrée salads or 4 as side salads

¾ cup pecans

2 ripe peaches

4 cups baby spinach

½ cup sour cream, mayonnaise, or plain low-fat yogurt

¼ cup sugar

2 tablespoons cider vinegar or fresh lemon juice

2 teaspoons poppy seeds

Preheat the oven to 350°F.

Arrange the pecans in a single layer on a baking sheet and toast for 7 to 10 minutes, until they just begin to darken. Remove from the oven and set aside to cool. Coarsely chop the pecans.

Peel the peaches (or not; this is an optional step) and slice them into 2-inch wedges. (You can grill the peaches, either on an outdoor grill or a preheated grill pan if you'd like: Toss the peach wedges with 1½ teaspoons olive oil and season with salt and pepper. Grill over high heat, turning once, until the peaches are lightly browned, about 3 minutes; let cool before using.) Place the peaches in a large bowl. Add the spinach and chopped pecans.

Make the dressing: In a small bowl, whisk together the sour cream, sugar, vinegar, and poppy seeds until thoroughly combined. (Alternately, combine all the ingredients in a jar with a lid and shake until combined.)

Just before serving, toss the salad with the dressing until the spinach leaves are evenly coated.

Grilled Hickory-Smoked Summer Squash and Zucchini Salad

This is an extremely easy dish to make, a great side to accompany any grilled or smoked main course. I especially like the fact that this salad combines hot grilled veggies with cool lettuce—a grilled salad is the effect, and the vegetables have a gently charred appeal. Good looking and good eating, my favorite.

Serves 4 as an appetizer or 6 as a side dish

4 red or orange bell peppers
6 small summer squash (about 1¾ pounds), sliced lengthwise ½ inch thick
1 large unpeeled sweet onion, cut in half lengthwise
2 medium zucchini, sliced lengthwise ½ inch thick
1 cup Only Rub (page 22)
1 tablespoon red wine vinegar
2 tablespoons extra-virgin olive oil
One 1-pound head romaine lettuce, leaves torn
Salt and freshly ground black pepper

If you've got a charcoal or gas grill going, grill the bell peppers on it for about 5 minutes per side, until the skins are blistered and charred. Alternatively, char the bell peppers under a preheated broiler. Transfer the bell peppers to a medium bowl, cover with plastic wrap, and let steam for 20 minutes. Peel, core, and seed the bell peppers and cut them into 1-inch-wide strips.

Generously brush the squash slices, onion pieces, and zucchini slices with the rub, reserving 1 tablespoon for the dressing. Grill or broil the vegetables for 20 minutes, or until the squash and zucchini are tender and the onion halves are charred and tender. Carefully peel the onion halves and cut them into 1-inch slices.

In a large bowl, whisk the vinegar with the reserved 1 tablespoon rub; slowly whisk in the olive oil until emulsified. Add the lettuce, season with salt and pepper, and toss to combine. Transfer the lettuce to a serving platter and arrange the grilled vegetables on top. Serve immediately.

Mexican-Style Grilled Corn

Roasted corn on the cob brushed with butter, coated in spices, and rolled in cheese. Do I need to say anything else? This is not only fun to eat; it's fun to make and a guaranteed crowd pleaser.

Serves 4 as a side dish

4 ears of corn

2 tablespoons Only Rub (page 22)

¼ cup mayonnaise

1 chipotle chile in adobo sauce,
   finely chopped

1½ teaspoons snipped chives, optional

2 tablespoons extra-virgin olive oil

¼ cup grated Mexican cojita cheese
   or Parmesan cheese

Lime wedges for serving

Preheat the smoker or charcoal grill to medium-high heat. Alternatively, preheat the oven the 425°F.

Peel back the cornhusks, leaving them attached. Discard the silk. Season the corn with 1 tablespoon of the rub. Replace the husks, wrap each ear in foil, transfer to an aluminum pan, and roast, covered, for about 30 minutes, until just tender.

Alternately, if you're short on time, you can cook the corn in the microwave: Don't shuck them and don't wrap them in foil; microwave on high for 8 minutes. Rotate the cobs a quarter turn and microwave for 8 more minutes. Turn the cobs again and microwave for another 8 minutes. Remove the corn from the microwave and run briefly under cool water. Shuck the ears leaving the husks attached; the silk comes off easily now.

In a bowl, whisk the remaining 1 tablespoon rub with the mayonnaise, chipotle, and chives, if using. Add the olive oil and whisk until smooth.

Heat a charcoal grill (see page 4) or gas grill (see page 5) to medium-high heat.

Peel back the cornhusks, leaving them attached. Brush the corn with half of the mayonnaise mixture. Using the husks as a handle, grill the corn until lightly charred, about 3 to 5 minutes. Brush each ear with the remaining mayonnaise and roll it in the cheese. Serve the corn immediately, with lime wedges alongside.

Smoked Potatoes

When you're already smoking something, why not make your whole dinner out on the grill? The advantage of smoking potatoes instead of baking them is that the potato skins take on a deep earthy flavor that the oven just can't match.

Serves 4

4 large baking potatoes, preferably russets
3 tablespoons unsalted butter, melted
1 tablespoon Only Rub (page 22)
Favorite toppings, such as homemade bacon bits, aged cheddar cheese, sour cream, and butter

Prepare a smoker with soaked wood chips and heat it to 325°F (see page 6). Alternatively, prepare a charcoal grill (see page 7) or gas grill (see page 8) for smoking and heat it to medium heat.

Wash the potatoes thoroughly, scrubbing any dirt from their skin, and dry them with paper towels. Prick each potato with a fork (so that steam can escape during the baking and the potato doesn't explode). Brush the potatoes all over with the melted butter and season with the rub.

Place the potatoes in the smoker, cover, and smoke the potatoes until they are cooked through, 1 to 1¼ hours; the skins will be crisp and the potatoes will yield to the touch and feel soft in the center.

Wrap the potatoes in aluminum foil to keep them warm until ready to serve. Serve with your favorite toppings.

Pitmaster-Style Grilled Veggie Kebabs

Ribs, brisket, pork shoulder, whole hog: These are the main focal points of the pit-master. Grilled veggie kebabs? You're thinking: *no way?* I'm here to tell you that these are not thin and prissy little sticks of soggy vegetables. My veggie kebabs are full flavored thanks to the hickory rub, made substantial thanks to the smoked potatoes. They're manly enough to be as delicious as they are good for you.

NOTE: If using wooden skewers, soak them in water for 30 minutes before using to prevent them from burning on the grill.

Serves 4 as a side dish

1 pound small new potatoes
Salt
1 tablespoon olive oil
1 large red or green bell pepper, cored, seeded, and cut into 1-inch dice
1 medium sweet onion, cut lengthwise into 4 wedges
3 small zucchini, cut diagonally into 1½-inch-thick pieces
1 pint cherry tomatoes
1 cup Only Marinade (page 21)

Heat a charcoal grill (see page 4) or gas grill (see page 5) to medium-high heat. Alternatively, preheat the broiler.

Prepare the potatoes: Place the potatoes in a large saucepan and add cold water to cover. Add salt and bring to a boil. Reduce the heat and simmer until just tender; about 20 minutes, and drain. Cut the potatoes into wedges and drizzle with the olive oil. Toss well and set aside.

Assemble the kebabs by evenly divding the vegetables, including the reserved new potatoes, and threading them onto metal or wooden skewers. Brush the kebabs generously with the marinade, reserving about 2 tablespoons.

continued

Place the kebabs on the grill and grill uncovered, brushing a few times with the remaining marinade, until the vegetables are tender and lightly charred, 4 to 5 minutes per side. (If broiling, broil for about 2 minutes, brush the kebabs with remaining marinade, and broil for an additional 2 to 3 minutes, until the vegetables are tender.) Serve immediately alongside grilled chicken, steak, or other barbecued main course.

Smoky Collard Greens

This is the fastest way I know to make old-fashioned stewed collards, which benefit tremendously from the addition of bacon's smoky essence. (What doesn't?) My tip for delicious collards is to make them a day ahead of time: This is one of those dishes that is just so much more delicious when it's had time to sit for a day or so before serving so that the flavors marry and intensify.

Serves 6 to 8 as a side dish

2 bunches collard greens, stemmed
2 teaspoons vegetable oil
½ Vidalia or other sweet onion, sliced
3 slices bacon, cut crosswise into ¼-inch strips
2 tablespoons cider vinegar
1 cup chicken stock
Salt

Working in batches, stack the greens and cut them crosswise into 2-inch-thick strips. Gather the strips and cut them crosswise into 2-inch pieces. Transfer to a large bowl of cold water and swish to remove any grit. Transfer the greens to a colander using a slotted spoon; drain. Repeat until the greens are free of grit.

Heat the vegetable oil in a very large skillet over medium-high heat. Add the onions and bacon and cook until the onions are translucent, about 4 minutes. Add the greens and cook, stirring, until the greens begin to wilt and are reduced in volume.

Raise the heat to high and add the vinegar. Cook, scraping up the browned bits from the bottom of the skillet, until the vinegar has evaporated, about 1 minute.

Pour in the stock, reduce the heat, cover, and simmer until the greens are just tender, 12 to 14 minutes. Season with salt. Cool, cover, and refrigerate overnight. Reheat over low heat and serve alongside your main course.

Barbecue Jalapeño-Cheddar Hushpuppies

I like to serve old-fashioned Georgia-style hushpuppies, simply spiced with onion powder. They're good, but they're very traditional. When I feel like spicing things up, I mix the classic combo of jalapeños and Cheddar into my batter and sprinkle the puppies with rub when they're finished. These are so delicious and addictive that you can even serve them as an appetizer, alongside some Slow-Smoked Barbecue Cherry Tomatoes (page 256) or ketchup if you like.

Makes about 16 hushpuppies, enough to serve 4 as a side dish

1½ cups yellow cornmeal
½ cup all-purpose flour
1 teaspoon baking powder
1 teaspoon salt
1 teaspoon Louisiana-style hot sauce
¼ cup minced yellow onion
2 jalapeño peppers, seeded and minced
3 ounces grated sharp Cheddar cheese (about 1 cup)
2 large eggs, beaten
½ cup milk
Vegetable oil for deep-frying
1 tablespoon Only Rub (page 22)

Combine the cornmeal, flour, baking powder, salt, hot sauce, onions, jalapeños, and Cheddar in a medium bowl and mix well. Add the eggs and milk and mix again to combine; the batter will be lumpy.

Heat 4 inches of vegetable oil in a large, heavy, deep pot or electric fryer to 360°F. Drop the batter into the oil a heaping tablespoon at a time, frying 6 at a time. When the hush-puppies pop to the surface, roll them around in the oil with a slotted spoon to brown them evenly. Remove and drain on paper towels. Sprinkle with the rub and serve immediately.

Barbecue Smoked Cabbage

This side dish is perfect to cook when you've already got your smoker going (it's also perfect because my wife, Faye, came up with the recipe!). You can easily prepare the head of cabbage and toss it on right along with the meat you're smoking and time it so that the main course and its side will be ready at the same time. Cabbage cooked this way is like a cross between coleslaw and sauerkraut, but with a terrific smoke flavor.

Serves 4

1 head green cabbage
1 tablespoon salt
1 teaspoon freshly ground black pepper
1 teaspoon garlic powder
1 teaspoon onion powder
½ cup (1 stick) unsalted butter

Using a sharp knife, core the cabbage, carving out the tough white bottom. Rinse the cored cabbage and pull off any wilted leaves. Sprinkle the salt, pepper, garlic powder, and onion powder into the hollowed center. Place the stick of butter inside the center, where the core was removed and over the spices you just sprinkled.

Wrap the head of cabbage in aluminum foil so that the core end is up. Using more foil, form a base to keep the cabbage upright. Place the wrapped cabbage on the smoker. Cover and smoke for 4 to 6 hours, until the cabbage is soft. Unwrap and discard any blackened leaves. Cut into quarters and serve alongside the smoked meat of your choice.

Slow-Smoked Barbecue Cherry Tomatoes

Make sure you cook these little tomatoes until blackened bits appear on them: This is the best indication of sweet and smoky flavor. You can eat these tomatoes alongside any barbecue, but they're also great to have on hand as an ingredient. (You can store them in an airtight container in the refrigerator for up to a week.) You can use them to make smoky salsa or robust marinara sauce, or strew them on top of a cheeseburger.

Serves 4 as a side dish

2½ pints cherry tomatoes
1 tablespoon olive oil
1 teaspoon kosher salt
2 teaspoons Only Rub (page 22)
4 to 6 whole garlic cloves

Prepare a smoker with soaked wood chips and heat it to 250°F (see page 6). Alternatively, prepare a charcoal grill (see page 7) or gas grill (see page 8) for smoking and heat it to medium-high heat.

In a large bowl, gently toss the tomatoes with the olive oil, salt, rub, and garlic. Pour the tomatoes into a long, shallow aluminum pan. Place the pan on the smoker, cover, and smoke the tomatoes for 1 hour to 1½ hours, until they're bursting, juicy, and soft. Let cool for about 10 minutes, then serve the tomatoes alongside a smoked or grilled meat dish.

Make it in a stovetop smoker: Soak 1 cup wood chips in water for 30 minutes. Line a large wok with aluminum foil. Place the soaked wood chips in the bottom of the wok on top of the foil. Place a metal rack, such a small baking rack, on top of the chips. Place the pan of tomatoes on top of this rack and smoke the tomatoes for 1 hour to 1½ hours, low heat, until they're bursting, juicy, and soft. Let cool for about 10 minutes, then serve the tomatoes alongside a smoked or grilled meat dish.

Vidalia Onion Relish

What's this doing in a chapter about salads and side dishes? In the South, relish isn't just something you put on your hotdog (although this sweet onion relish happens to be excellent on a grilled hotdog or bratwurst). Our relishes are tangy and have a bit of crunch, meant to be enjoyed alongside grilled or smoked meats and veggies. It's perfect to serve with a thick and juicy steak.

Makes about 2½ cups

1 small Vidalia or other sweet onion, cut in half and thinly sliced
1 small red onion, cut in half and thinly sliced
1 cup white wine vinegar or other mild vinegar
½ cup sugar
1 tablespoon Only Rub (page 22)

In a medium bowl, combine the sweet and red onions; add just enough ice water to cover. Soak for 30 minutes, changing the ice water once about halfway through. Drain the onions well and return them to the bowl.

In a medium saucepan, combine the vinegar, sugar, and rub and bring to a boil, stirring until the sugar is dissolved. Pour the mixture over the onions and set aside to cool, tossing occasionally. You can store the relish in a jar, refrigerated, for up to 1 week.

Grilled Sweet Onion and Green Tomato Chowchow

Chowchow is a Southern staple, a special kind of relish, often pickled, and always containing tomatoes. It's piquant and tangy, really nice with brisket or chicken (or even mixed into a classic chicken salad). And, as you might expect, it is great on burgers and hotdogs.

NOTE: If using wooden skewers, soak them in water for 30 minutes before using to prevent them from burning on the grill. Also soak the toothpicks.

Serves 4 as a side dish or condiment

2 Vidalia or other sweet onions, sliced ½ inch thick
2 jalapeño peppers
Extra-virgin olive oil for brushing
1 cup coarsely chopped green tomatoes
½ cup cider vinegar
¼ cup plus 2 tablespoons light brown sugar
½ cup grainy mustard
1 teaspoon Only Rub (page 22)
1 teaspoon cornstarch dissolved in 2 teaspoons water
Salt and freshly ground black pepper

Heat a charcoal grill (see page 4) or gas grill (see page 5) to medium heat.

Skewer each onion slice with a toothpick and thread the jalapeños on a skewer. Brush the onions and jalapeños with olive oil, cover, and grill until charred but still slightly crisp, about 10 minutes. Remove the toothpicks and skewer. When cool enough to handle, coarsely chop the onions. Peel and chop the jalapeños.

In a medium saucepan, combine the tomatoes, vinegar, brown sugar, mustard, and rub; place over medium heat and bring to a simmer. Add the chopped onions and jalapeños and cook, stirring frequently, until the liquid is reduced by one quarter to one third, about 12 minutes. Stir the cornstarch mixture; add it to the pan and cook, stirring occasionally, until slightly thickened, about 2 minutes. Remove the chow-chow from the heat, season with salt and pepper, and let cool. Serve at room temperature with your grilled meat dish. The chowchow can be refrigerated, covered, for up to 1 week.

eleven

DESSERT

CHOCOLATE CAKE ON THE GRILL

GRILLED SKILLET APPLE PIE

FRIED PEACH PIES

GRILLED BANANAS AND MAPLE RUM SAUCE

GRILLED STRAWBERRY COBBLER

GRILLED PEACHES AND BOURBON CREAM

S'MORES CHEESECAKE

GEORGIA PEACH ICE CREAM

GEORGIA PEANUT PEANUT BUTTER ICE CREAM

GRILLED POUND CAKE

GRILLED BANANA-CHOCOLATE BOATS

The only options in most people's minds when it comes to desserts and barbecue are two things: banana pudding and peach cobbler. That's because those are the two desserts you'll likely find in any barbecue joint worth its salt that wants to bother with something sweet—some just skip dessert altogether. I love both; I just wish they weren't relegated to an afterthought. But I also know well that not only are these two not always the easiest to make for a busy weeknight mealtime, it's also not a bad idea to have a few more options up your sleeve.

A lot of the desserts here are designed—by me, the winningest man in barbecue—to be cooked on your grill or smoker, to make the most of your heat while it's hot. Yes, you read that right. These are desserts made on your grill. They aren't baked in your oven and then brought to the table as they belong with the smoked meats. These are barbecue dishes that happen to be sweet. And they are as delicious and deserving of a spot on the table as anything else.

A few notable exceptions: I love S'mores Cheesecake (page 278), and you can make it the day before you serve it. Simple, right? And of course my ice creams: perfect to cleanse and cool the palate after an afternoon of barbecue.

What I like in a dessert is something to leave a good taste in my mouth, a little bite of something sweet to finish. I want a dessert that tastes good, that's easy to make, and doesn't require the worriation that comes with traditional baking.

What you can expect in my collection of desserts is mostly dressed-up versions of campfire classics—and the chocolate and marshmallow-stuffed banana boats are actually straight out of the Cub Scouts campouts. Some of these desserts are good enough for steakhouses, like the grilled bananas with the maple rum sauce, but not a single one of them is hard to make or is something that I'd consider beyond the reach of any backyard barbecue enthusiast. A little bit of sweet goes a long way in making me happy. And I bet you're just the same.

Chocolate Cake on the Grill

This big ole chocolate Bundt cake gets the pitmaster treatment when I cook it in on the grill and allow the flavors of smoke to permeate it just enough to make it extra rich and earthy. (When you think about it, what's a grill but a glorified smoke- or charcoal-fired outdoor oven anyway?) You don't have to bother with the glaze if you don't want to, but if you're having company it adds a slightly fancier touch. And if you are real adventurous, top the glaze with crumbled bacon—it really enhances that smoky flavor.

Serves 10 to 12

Cake

¾ cup (1½ sticks) plus 1 tablespoon unsalted butter, softened

2 cups all-purpose flour

½ cup unsweetened cocoa powder

2 teaspoons baking powder

½ teaspoon baking soda

½ teaspoon salt

1 cup plus 2 tablespoons sugar

3 large eggs

3 ounces semisweet chocolate, melted and cooled

2 teaspoons pure vanilla extract

1½ cups sour cream

Glaze

½ cup sugar

¼ cup water

1 tablespoon unsweetened cocoa powder

1 teaspoon pure vanilla extract

Optional: shredded coconut, toasted; whipped cream and fruit; or crumbled bacon.

continued on page 267

Make the cake: Heat a charcoal grill (see page 4) or gas grill (see page 5) to medium heat. Alternatively, preheat the oven to 350°F.

Generously grease an 8-cup Bundt pan with 1 tablespoon of the butter and set aside.

In a medium bowl, sift the flour with the cocoa, baking powder, baking soda, and salt. In a large bowl using an electric mixer, beat the remaining ¾ cup butter until creamy. Add the sugar and beat until light and fluffy. Add the eggs, one at a time, beating well after each addition. Add the melted chocolate and vanilla and beat until the batter is smooth. Beat in the dry ingredients in 3 batches, alternating with the sour cream.

Scrape the batter into the prepared pan and smooth the surface.

Place the cake pan on the grill and cover, or place it in the oven; grill or bake for 45 minutes to 1 hour, until a skewer inserted in the center comes out with moist crumbs attached. Remove from the grill or oven and let the cake cool in the pan completely, about 1 hour.

Meanwhile, make the glaze: In a medium saucepan, combine the sugar and the water and bring to a boil over medium heat; stir to dissolve the sugar. Remove from the heat, whisk in the cocoa powder and vanilla, and let cool.

Invert the cake onto a serving platter. Brush a thin layer of the glaze over the cake and let dry slightly. Repeat 3 more times, letting the glaze dry slightly before brushing the cake again. Top with toasted coconut or crumbled bacon, if you're using. Cut into wedges and serve with whipped cream and fruit if you like. It also goes well with Georgia Peanut Peanut Butter Ice Cream (page 281).

Grilled Skillet Apple Pie

I buy premade piecrusts for my skillet apple pie; they're so easy to lay into a cast-iron skillet, and from there so easy to set onto the grill or smoker and bake. I like the sweeter apples like Golden Delicious for this pie as opposed to the tart ones like Granny Smiths, but you can use whichever you like best.

Serves 12

3½ pounds Golden Delicious or other apples, peeled, cored, and cut in half
1 tablespoon vegetable oil
½ cup plus 1 tablespoon sugar
3 tablespoons cornstarch
1 tablespoon fresh lemon juice
One 15-ounce package rolled refrigerated unbaked piecrust (2 crusts)
Cooking spray
1 large egg
1 tablespoon water

Heat a charcoal grill (see page 10) or gas grill (see page 8) set up for indirect heat to medium-high heat.

Brush the apple halves with the vegetable oil. Place the apple halves cut side down on a grill rack directly over the coals for 3 minutes uncovered, or until lightly browned. Remove the apple halves from the heat to a bowl and set aside until cool enough to handle, then cut the apple halves into wedges.

In a large bowl, toss the apples with ½ cup of the sugar, the cornstarch, and the lemon juice, and set aside.

On a lightly floured surface, roll each prepared crust to a 12-inch diameter. Coat a 9½- to 10-inch cast-iron skillet with cooking spray. Line the skillet with one of the crusts with the dough coming three quarters of the way up the sides of the pan. Place

continued on page 270

the apple mixture into the crust in the skillet. With a sharp knife, cut several slits in the center of the second crust to vent steam. Place the second crust over the pie filling. Tuck any extra dough at the edges between the side of the skillet and the bottom crust. Crimp the edges with a fork.

In a small bowl, lightly beat the egg with the water. Brush the pie with the egg wash, then sprinkle the top with the remaining 1 tablespoon sugar.

Place the skillet on the grill rack over the cool side of the grill. Cover and grill for 1½ to 2 hours, until the crust is golden and the filling is bubbly, rotating once halfway through the grilling. Cool the pie on a wire rack for 30 to 40 minutes before slicing.

Fried Peach Pies

The Varsity, Atlanta's prototypical fast-food restaurant situated right downtown, is famous for its individual handheld fried peach pies. Folks down here in middle Georgia have been making these forever because they're easy to hold and delicious.

Serves 6

½ cup (1 stick) plus 1 tablespoon unsalted butter, softened
3 tablespoons sugar
¼ teaspoon salt
1 large egg
1½ cups all-purpose flour
2 tablespoons ice water
2 cups thinly sliced ripe fresh peaches
¼ cup peach preserves
Vegetable oil for frying
Vanilla ice cream for serving, optional

In the bowl of a stand mixer, beat together ½ cup of the butter, 2½ tablespoons of the sugar, and the salt on medium speed for about 3 minutes. Add the egg and beat for about 30 seconds until well combined and slightly thickened. Add the flour and water and beat just to combine, about 15 seconds. Turn off the machine, scrape down the sides of the bowl, and beat again for 10 seconds. Scoop out the dough with your hands and form it into a 1-inch-thick disk. Cover in plastic wrap and refrigerate for at least 1 hour and as long as 4 hours.

Melt the remaining 1 tablespoon butter in a medium saucepan over medium-high heat. Add the peaches and the remaining ½ tablespoon sugar and cook until the sugar is dissolved, about 2 minutes. Add the preserves and cook, stirring constantly, until the peaches soften and the preserves melt, about 3 minutes. Remove from the heat and set aside to cool.

(continued on page 273)

On a lightly floured surface, divide the dough into 6 equal pieces and roll out each one. Place the circles on a baking sheet lined with parchment paper. Spread about ¼ cup of the cooled cooked peaches on half of each circle. Fold the other half over the filling and crimp the edges securely with a fork. Refrigerate the pies for at least 20 minutes before frying.

When ready to cook, preheat the oven to 200°F.

Pour enough vegetable oil to come about 2½ inches up the sides of a heavy 4-quart saucepan or cast-iron skillet and heat the oil to 350°F. Fry the pies 2 or 3 at a time, being careful not to crowd the pan, for 1½ to 2 minutes per batch, until golden brown. Drain the pies on paper towels. Keep the pies warm in the oven until all of the pies are fried. Serve the pies immediately, topped with vanilla ice cream if you like.

Grilled Bananas and Maple Rum Sauce

This is a barbecue guy's version of bananas Foster, the beautiful and fancy flaming banana dessert made famous in New Orleans. It's normally made in a skillet on the stove, but it's very easy to make on the grill, and then you don't have to worry about setting anything on fire in the process. You can substitute plantains for the bananas if you're feeling exotic, and if you're not already firing up the grill, you can bake the bananas or cook them in a sauté pan with a little oil until they become dark golden and soft.

Serves 4

½ cup maple syrup

2 tablespoons dark rum

2 large very ripe bananas

1 tablespoon vegetable oil

2 cups vanilla ice cream or Georgia Peanut Peanut Butter Ice Cream (page 281)

Heat a charcoal grill (see page 4) or gas grill (see page 5) to medium heat or preheat the oven to 350°F.

In a small saucepan, combine the maple syrup and rum and heat over low heat, stirring, just until bubbles begin to form on the surface. Do not let it boil. Remove from the heat and set aside. Warm the sauce gently again just before serving.

Peel the bananas and make a vertical slice down the center of each. Brush the bananas with the vegetable oil; this will prevent them from sticking to the grill.

Place the bananas flat side down and grill until dark golden and soft, 3 to 4 minutes. Turn the bananas and grill for a few more minutes, until the bananas are soft throughout and dark golden on the second side, about 4 minutes more. (If you are making them in the oven, put the slit bananas on a baking sheet, place in the oven, and bake for 5 minutes.)

Remove the bananas from the grill and slice them into bite-size chunks.

Scoop ½ cup of ice cream in each of 4 bowls. Top each with a few sliced grilled bananas and drizzle a little of the warm maple rum sauce over the top.

Grilled Strawberry Cobbler

I love pie, but I sure don't love the bother and worriation of making a crust. That's why I like cobblers, because you get the sweet fresh filling of a fruit pie, but all you have to make is the topping. And when I can make one on an already-hot smoker, it's even better. The ginger in here gives the strawberries a little extra bite; that's my secret ingredient.

Serves 6

5 cups sliced fresh strawberries

½ cup granulated sugar

1 tablespoon quick-cooking tapioca

¼ teaspoon salt

2 teaspoons grated fresh ginger,
   or ¾ teaspoon ground ginger

¾ cup crushed shortbread cookies
   (about 12 cookies)

⅓ cup all-purpose flour

3 tablespoons packed light brown sugar

2 tablespoons unsalted butter

Whipped cream or ice cream for serving,
   optional

Make the filling: In a large bowl, combine the strawberries, granulated sugar, tapioca, salt, and ginger. Pour the mixture into a 2-quart disposable foil pan. Cover the pan tightly with aluminum foil.

Prepare a smoker with soaked wood chips and heat it to 275°F (see page 6). Alternatively, prepare a charcoal grill (see page 7) or gas grill (see page 8) for smoking and heat it to medium heat.

Make the topping: In the bowl of a food processor, combine the crushed shortbread cookies, flour, and brown sugar. Pulse a few times to combine. Add the butter and pulse until the butter is in small bits about the size of a pea and the topping has the consistency of coarsely ground meal; set aside.

Place the foil pan on a rack in the center of the smoker. Cover and smoke for 30 minutes. Uncover, sprinkle the topping evenly over fruit mixture, and cover again. Smoke for 10 to 15 minutes more, until the mixture is bubbly and the fruit has thickened. Cool the cobbler on a wire rack for 20 minutes. Serve warm, topped with whipped cream or ice cream, if you like.

Grilled Peaches and Bourbon Cream

As a bona fide Georgia peach myself, I'm well acquainted with the classic combination of peaches and cream. This is a riff on that theme, only I'm warming the fruit with the smokiness of the grill and goosing my cream with bourbon. And it's a really good idea to do those two things.

Serves 4

½ cup light brown sugar
½ cup (1 stick) unsalted butter
1 teaspoon ground cinnamon
4 large peaches, sliced into ½-inch wedges
1¼ cups heavy cream
2 tablespoons confectioners' sugar
1 tablespoon bourbon

Heat a charcoal grill (see page 4) or gas grill (see page 5) to medium-high heat.

Make the glaze: Combine the brown sugar, butter, and cinnamon in a medium, heavy saucepan and bring to a boil over high heat. Reduce the heat to medium and briskly simmer the glaze, stirring constantly, until thick and syrupy, 4 to 6 minutes. Remove the pan from the heat.

Place the peaches on the grill and grill, uncovered, until browned and tender, 2 to 4 minutes, basting them with the glaze. Transfer the peaches to a platter or individual dessert plates.

Make the bourbon cream: In a large chilled metal bowl using an electric mixer, beat the cream until soft peaks form. Add the confectioners' sugar and bourbon and beat until stiff peaks form. Top the grilled peaches with the whipped cream and any remaining glaze and serve immediately.

S'mores Cheesecake

I love s'mores, and I like to eat them when I'm sitting around a pit all night teaching my students the old traditions of barbecue at my cooking school. But I like to eat them other times too, and not have to stand in front of a hot fire to do so. Hence this recipe. Here's the secret to not cracking the top of a cheesecake: It should be removed from the oven when it is not completely set (the residual heat will cook it through without overcooking and causing the dreaded crack). Now you know. And you know what? If the top of your cheesecake cracks, cover it up with heaps of freshly whipped cream and no one will be the wiser.

Serves 12 to 16

1¼ cups graham cracker crumbs
3 tablespoons granulated sugar
¼ cup plus 2 tablespoons unsalted butter, melted
Three 8-ounce packages cream cheese, softened
1 cup packed light brown sugar
⅓ cup marshmallow creme
1 tablespoon pure vanilla extract
4 large eggs
¼ teaspoon ground cinnamon
1 cup milk chocolate chips
Whipped cream for serving

Preheat the oven to 425°F and generously grease a 10-inch springform pan.

In a medium bowl, combine the graham cracker crumbs, granulated sugar, and melted butter. Reserve ½ cup of the mixture, and pour the rest into the bottom of the prepared pan. Press the crumbs into the bottom of the pan to form an even layer. Bake for 5 minutes, or until the crust is light golden brown (it will be darker at the edges).

In large bowl using an electric mixer, beat the cream cheese on medium speed, scraping down the sides occasionally, until smooth. Add the brown sugar, marshmallow creme, and vanilla, and beat until smooth. Beat in the eggs, one at a time, beating for 1 minute after each addition. Beat in the cinnamon.

Sprinkle the chocolate chips over the crust and pour the batter over the chips.

Place the cake pan in a roasting pan and pour enough hot water into the pan to come halfway up the sides of the pan. Bake the cheesecake for 15 minutes, then reduce the oven temperature to 225°F. Bake for 55 minutes longer, or until the cheesecake is set around the edge and the center is almost set but just slightly wiggly. Remove from the oven. Remove the cheesecake from the water bath and cool on a wire rack to room temperature. Cover loosely with foil and refrigerate for at least 3 hours or overnight.

When ready to serve, release the springform. Top the cheesecake with whipped cream, sprinkle the reserved graham cracker crumbs over the top, slice, and serve.

Georgia Peach Ice Cream

The single best dessert on the Fourth of July, when it's hot as hell outside and you've been smoking ribs all day, is some fresh peach ice cream. This ice cream isn't what I'd call "peach flavored": It's actually more like pure vanilla ice cream, extra custardy and rich, that's flavored with chunks of fresh ripe peaches. That's the way peach ice cream ought to be.

Makes 1 generous quart

3 large egg yolks
¾ cup packed light brown sugar
1½ cups heavy cream
1½ cups whole milk
2 tablespoons fresh lemon juice
1 teaspoon pure vanilla extract
3 large peaches, such as the world's best Georgia peaches, peeled, pitted, and cut into bite-size chunks

In a large bowl, whisk together the egg yolks and brown sugar. In a large saucepan, bring the cream and milk to a simmer over low heat. Whisking constantly, slowly pour the hot milk mixture into the egg yolk mixture until combined. Return to the saucepan and cook over low heat for 3 to 5 minutes, stirring constantly, until the custard has thickened enough to coat the back of a spoon.

Strain the custard through a fine-mesh strainer set over a bowl. Let cool completely. Stir in the lemon juice and vanilla. Cover and refrigerate the mixture overnight.

Churn the custard in an ice cream maker according to the manufacturer's instructions, adding the peach chunks halfway through churning. Store in the freezer until ready to serve.

Georgia Peanut Peanut Butter Ice Cream

Peanuts are another native Georgia crop, and I love their saltiness when added to sweets. This ice cream has both peanuts and peanut butter mixed in, giving it lots of texture and crunch in addition to creamy richness. It's excellent on top of anything chocolate or with some chocolate sauce on top.

Makes 1 generous quart

2 cups heavy cream
1 cup half-and-half
¾ cup sugar
1 teaspoon pure vanilla extract
⅓ cup crunchy-style peanut butter, preferably naturally ground
1 cup coarsely chopped salted peanuts

In a large bowl, combine the heavy cream, half-and-half, sugar, and vanilla and stir until well blended. Pour into an ice cream maker and churn according to the manufacturer's instructions. Halfway through churning, add the peanut butter to the mixture one spoonful at a time, churning to combine. When the ice cream is almost completely churned, add the peanuts. Store in the freezer until ready to serve.

Grilled Pound Cake

Obviously you don't have to actually make the pound cake for this recipe to work. If you've got a good local bakery, or even one called Sara Lee, you can take a store-bought one and make a killer dessert on your smoker or grill, heating it as directed below and adding some toppings. If you'd like the pride of making your own, here's an easy way to do it.

Makes one 9-inch pound cake; serves 8

2 cups (4 sticks) unsalted butter, softened
1 pound confectioners' sugar, 3¾ cups
6 large eggs
2½ cups all-purpose flour
1 teaspoon pure vanilla extract
Favorite toppings such as fresh whipped cream, salted Georgia peanuts, and
    chocolate sauce

Preheat the oven to 350°F and generously grease a 9 by 5-inch loaf pan.

In a large bowl using an electric mixer, cream the butter and confectioners' sugar until thoroughly combined, pale yellow, and ribbony. Add the eggs, one egg at a time, beating well after each addition. Beat in the flour, then add the vanilla. Scrape the batter into the prepared pan and bake for about 1 hour, or until golden brown and a toothpick inserted in the center comes out clean. Cool completely on a wire rack before turning out onto a plate.

When you are ready to grill, cut the cake into 8 equal slices.

Heat a charcoal grill (see page 4) or gas grill (see page 5) to medium-high heat.

Place the cake slices on the grill and grill the slices uncovered for 2 to 4 minutes, until toasted and heated through, turning once halfway through the grilling.

Serve the grilled cake slices warm with your favorite toppings.

Grilled Banana-Chocolate Boats

This recipe is based on an old-fashioned classic campfire dessert known far and wide to Boy Scouts of all stripes (even lapsed ones like me). It's simple, homey, rustic, and delicious: a great way to end a barbecue. And it just don't get any easier than this.

Serves 4

4 large bananas
1 cup chocolate chips
4 tablespoons mini marshmallows

Heat a charcoal grill (see page 4) or gas grill (see page 5) to medium heat.

Split the bananas lengthwise about ½ inch deep, leaving ½ inch, still in their skins, at both ends: You're creating a boat to hold the ingredients. Load each banana with ¼ cup of chocolate chips and 1 tablespoon mini marshmallows. Wrap individually in 10 by 8-inch squares of foil, then place on the grill, cover, and grill until the chocolate chips melt and the marshmallows are golden brown, 5 to 8 minutes. Open up and eat with a spoon.

acknowledgments

In putting together *Everyday Barbecue* for you, I had the support of the most important people in my life. I'd like to thank my wife, Faye, and my children, Kylie, Cory, David, and Michael. And my brothers, Tracy and Vince. And my pets, Lola, Bella, Winston, and Roxy, whom I adore. I would like to thank my longtime barbecue assistants, Nick and Eric. I also acknowledge the hard work and dedication of my Jack's Old South crew, Edd, Tim, TJ, Ross, and Tom. I want to thank my partners in crime who have helped me come so far, Super Agent Michael Psaltis, the best in the business, and the greatest food writer in the world, Kelly Alexander. I want to give a shout-out to the crew at my Pride and Joy restaurant in Miami: Mike, Paul, Chris, Jose, and Pablo. And finally I want to thank Rob, who builds some cool smokers.

—Myron Mixon

As a food journalist I've worked with a lot of chefs and cooks, and Myron Mixon has a special place in my heart. He truly walks it like he talks it and he's not just a barbecue champion, but also a world-class collaborator and a down-to-earth friend. I thank him for the opportunity to keep working together, and I thank his family for their warmth and diligence. Thank you to our editor, Ryan Doherty, who had the good sense to believe in Myron from the beginning, and to his team at Random House. Thank you to Super Agent Michael Psaltis, who has had my back for years. And thank you to my husband, Andrew, and our sons, Louis and Dylan, who love me anyway.

—Kelly Alexander

index

about the authors

MYRON MIXON was quite literarily born to barbecue. Raised in Vienna, Georgia, his father, Jack, owned a BBQ restaurant that Myron helped run. His parents started selling Jack's Old South BBQ Sauce, and after his father died in 1996, Myron thought that by entering competitions he could sell some sauce. He was hooked. He is the author of the *New York Times* bestselling cookbook, *Smokin' with Myron Mixon;* the star of Destination America's *BBQ Pitmasters* and *Pitmasters: Father vs. Son;* and the Chef/Owner of the Pride and Joy Bar-B-Que restaurants.

KELLY ALEXANDER, a James Beard Award–winning author, is a former editor at *Food & Wine* and *Saveur* magazines, and her work has appeared in the *New York Times,* the *New York Times Magazine, Gourmet,* and *Newsweek,* among others. She also teaches food writing at Duke, and is a graduate of Northwestern's Medill School of Journalism.